"The psalms have shaped the core of official Christian prayer for centuries, incorporated into the liturgy of the Word at the Eucharist and forming the content of the Church's daily morning and evening prayer. In this engaging and informative exploration of these great biblical prayers, James Chatham employs his skill as a scholar and a pastor to invite the lay reader to become part of the 'conversation' within the book of the Psalms, allowing the dynamic and sometime turbulent prayers of the psalmist to touch our own hearts."

—Donald Senior, CP
President Emeritus and Professor of New Testament
at Catholic Theological Union

"I read *Psalm Conversations* and felt like I was part of the discussion. The power of Jim's teachings transformed my faith. I recommend this book to anyone who is searching for understanding."

—Rosemarie Mucci, PhD
University Supervisor at Baldwin Wallace University

"For those of us who know and love the Psalms, James Chatham's book is a gift that offers new perspectives and new avenues for faithful appropriation. For those who don't know the Psalms, this book is a wonderful introduction! Chatham writes with a scholar's wisdom and a pastor's heart (he was a pastor for thirty-seven years), and he succeeds beautifully in showing how the psalmists speak to each other and to us in a way that we contemporary folk desperately need to hear. His exposition is clear; his many vignettes and stories are engaging; and each chapter's concluding 'Discussion Topics and Questions' make this a perfect resource for adult education that aims at helping us realize that we are 'accompanied always by God's great heart of love' (from the Preface)."

—Clint McCann
Evangelical Professor of Biblical Interpretation
Eden Theological Seminary
Saint Louis, Missouri

D1328098

"This book is simply beautiful. James Chatham manages to weave together explanatory notes on each psalm and its context along with stories from his own years in ministry. What emerges is a beautiful tapestry that is not yet finished. It requires our own connections—connections that begin to emerge in our reading and then more specifically through skillfully spun questions at the close of each chapter. As a teacher often called upon to help adults pray with the psalms and understand their source and meaning, this book will now be in my supply kit. As a Christian who wrestles with the ways God acts in our world, this book will become a companion."

    —Catherine (Cackie) Upchurch
    Little Rock Scripture Study director

Psalm Conversations

*Listening In as They Talk
with One Another*

James O. Chatham

LITURGICAL PRESS
Collegeville, Minnesota

www.litpress.org

1   2   3   4   5   6   7   8   9

Library of Congress Cataloging-in-Publication Data

Names: Chatham, James O., 1937– author.
Title: Psalm conversations : listening in as they talk with one another / James O. Chatham.
Description: Collegeville, Minnesota : Liturgical Press, 2018.
Identifiers: LCCN 2017058902 (print) I LCCN 2018025648 (ebook) I ISBN 9780814644843 (ebook) I ISBN 9780814644607
Subjects: LCSH: Bible. Psalms—Criticism, interpretation, etc.
Classification: LCC BS1430.52 (ebook) I LCC BS1430.52 .C4235 2018 (print) I DDC 223/.206—dc23
LC record available at https://lccn.loc.gov/2017058902

CONTENTS

PREFACE

Reading the Psalms Editors' Intention

If we are upright, honest people, life will reward us; if we are deceitful, dishonest people, life will punish us: Is this true? Should we teach it to our children? Or does the world actually work by some other moral formula? Psalms 1 and 73 struggle over the question. Our country is engaged in precisely the same struggle. The Psalms' insight is remarkable, unexpected, eye-opening.

How shall we relate to people who have wronged us viciously, people we basically despise? Should we banish such negative thoughts from our heads, cleanse ourselves of malevolence, be all-forgiving? Can you imagine pulling that off? Psalms 136, 137, and 138, heard together, speak a telling word.

What collective message do Psalms 8, 19, 24, 65, 90, 104, and 148 issue about the role of awe and wonder in our lives, the sensation of being in the presence of something vastly beyond our comprehension? What does each psalm contribute? And what, indeed, does Psalms as a whole book add? The result is a word often lost on modern ears.

Numerous biblical psalms engage in animated conversations with one another over what to us are everyday life issues. One psalm will state a point, another will question it or speak from a different angle, and another will add an entirely new dimension, all feeding the hearer (you and me) with larger and richer perspectives. The conversations among psalms are sometimes implicit, challenging us as we knit together a picture. But often they are quite clear, leaving no doubt.

Amid all the negative emotions that can reside in you and me, can we implant a spirit of profound thanksgiving, making us fundamentally grateful people? This is a running psalm conversation.

How are we to face our own sinfulness, the great flaw within the self—individual and communal? Modern society often does this very poorly, urging us to pretense and self-deception. Psalms 51 and 106 join other texts in a chorus of commentary.

What can it do for us to feel *accompanied by the Spirit*, that a Presence travels with us on our path? What are the great hazards in believing this?

How shall I conduct myself when I get exceedingly angry with God, when the cruelties and injustices of life are beyond explanation? Am I supposed to shut up, keep my emotions inside, be accepting and polite? Or is there a better way?

When major catastrophe strikes, a horrible disaster, how are we to handle the despair that easily sets over us?

What about the times when God seems silent, when fervent prayer gets no answer?

These are conversations the psalms carry on with one another. The purpose of this book is for us to listen in on several psalm conversations, to realize how contemporary they are, and to join them. You and I have had plenty of experience with life, and we can make valuable contributions. The ancients invite us into the conversation.

A major role of the Psalms is to show us that we are not alone, that we are accompanied by a great crowd of fellow travelers, past and present, very much like us. The world has changed enormously in the twenty-five hundred years since the book of Psalms was gathered—space exploration, the tech world, genetic research—but we humans have changed very little, still engaging in the same internal plots and scripts as we always have. That's why we encounter ourselves repeatedly in the psalm conversations.

Another major role of the Psalms is to deliberate and discern the ways of God in this world. How is God like or not like what we envision? We humans tend to want God to bestow upon us special favors from on high: victories in conquest, safety against danger, rain from the sky, food from the soil, babies from the womb, healing from illness, success in our endeavors. We also want God to grant to us and people like us an elevated status, as if we are chosen and set apart for privilege, "exceptional." The book of Psalms has an enormously larger view of God, *God transcendent* as well as *God immanent*, God far beyond our small human life-orbits as well as God our intimate, personal companion. This two-faceted theology, the book urges, is critical in discerning accurately God's relation to humanity. It, too, is the subject of psalm conversations.

A few years ago biblical interpreters began paying attention to what is called *the shape and shaping of the Psalms*. For years we had studied Psalms mostly in individual units, one document at a time. Now, we also wish to ask what the volume's compilers (editors) were saying by the content and arrangement of the book. What interchange do Psalms 22 and 23, Psalms 89 and 90, Psalms 105, 106, and 107 have with one another? How may Psalm 73 be nearly the center of the entire volume, focusing everything before and after? What message is delivered by the fact that the closing psalms in the book, 145–150, issue unbounded praise and adoration for God, amplifying the highly enigmatic, final verse of the much-distraught Psalm 89? What was the purpose behind the shaping, and how are we to interpret the shape? The inquiry has led to rich results!

The Torah—the first five books of the Bible—has been long revered in the Hebrew/Jewish tradition as the sacred record of God's acts in founding Israel and of God's instructions for ordering the nation's life. The history and the law: Torah. The creators of Psalms also divided their book into five units: Book I: Psalms 1–41; Book II: Psalms 42–72; Book III: Psalms 73–89; Book IV: Psalms 90–106; and Book V: Psalms 107–150. They almost certainly did this with parallel purpose. What was that purpose?

If the five books of the Torah present the event history of Israel, the five books of Psalms seem to present an internal/spiritual history of Israel: what took place in the nation's mind and soul. Historical occurrences are clearly reflected, but the major subject is the human interior: its rejoicing and lamentation, its faith and doubt. The soaring peaks and deep canyons of the heart as it makes its way through human life: that is Psalms. You and I discover, as generations before us have, enormous identity with our own experience.

The formation of the Psalms as a gathered collection probably took place around 525–500 BCE. In 587 BCE, Jerusalem and its holy temple had been destroyed by the invading Babylonian army. Many of the city's citizens had been deported into exile in refugee camps on the Euphrates River where they had remained for nearly fifty years. After 540 BCE, when Cyrus the Persian defeated Babylon, a great number of the refugees made their way back home and began rebuilding both the city and the temple. This "second temple" was completed and dedicated in 515 BCE.

The editors of the book of Psalms were creating what has been called "the hymnbook of the second temple," songs sung or chanted by worshipers approaching the holy site or offering sacrifices in the temple courts. It is likely that on a normal day the temple was alive with psalm singing accompanied by stringed instruments. The book of Psalms seems designed to voice what Israel had been through in its recent tumultuous decades, and, through it all, to proclaim a deep and abiding faith in God. If the Torah told the historical-event story of what led to the first Israel, the Psalms would tell the spiritual/ emotional story of what led to the second. From embattled kingship, through national disintegration and destruction, through bitter exile, and into restoration, the Psalms would track the nation's inner plight.

From what we are told by ancient sources, several thousand "psalms of David" were available for inclusion in the book. These 150 were, therefore, likely selected and arranged with purpose. Reading and interpreting that purpose is our point here.

And, one other factor. The Psalms editors were working with documents composed previously by other people and already in popular use. They probably felt constrained, therefore, to use whole psalms pretty much as they received them, not changing individual documents very much. Several psalms seem to have "exilic postscripts" (e.g., Psalm 51), verses at the end praying for national restoration, but there seems to be little other editing. As a result, one portion of a particular psalm may fit the editors' overall purpose while another portion of that same psalm does not. Both portions will have been included, however. The outcome may be confusing to us until we recall how the editors were working.

Who edited the Psalms? No one knows; there is no record. Three things are apparent, however. The editors knew music, attaching notations to their texts to guide their use by singers and music leaders. The editors also knew well the theological currents of their day, the Davidic covenant that was shattered by the destruction of Jerusalem, and the subsequent Deuteronomic covenant now emerging in the national consciousness (more on this in the chapters that follow). And, the editors knew intimately the internal struggles of their people, the mental turmoils of destruction and continued trauma. The editors had great insight and a message to bear, the purpose being to sustain both community and faith through a tumultuous time. This is what the book of Psalms is all about: faith through hard, hard struggle. Multitudes of believers have turned to the book for precisely that in the centuries since its collection.

I invite you, throughout this book, to immerse yourself in the mind, heart, and world of the Psalms editors, to get to know the editors intimately, and to realize that their world was very much like ours. They have vital things to say to us, much of which has been lost to modern ears. We need to hear! The editors' purpose is to build in us faith, to enable us to be accompanied always by God's great heart of love. Let us listen intently to the ancient wisdom!

I have designed this book as a dialogue between author and reader. I will set forth psalm data, state my own thoughts, pose questions, and ask you to deliberate and reply. Perhaps, sharing your conversation in a group will be most valuable. I have used these materials a number of times in lay Bible courses and elder hostels, and invariably class participants, from their experience, offer valuable input I would have missed. I hope you will do the same.

Special thanks to Rosemarie Mucci of Parma, Ohio, who took this course in a classroom and then, from her long interest in lay Bible study and her career as a teacher of teachers, provided invaluable comments in the preparation of this manuscript.

Also sincere thanks to Clint McCann, Evangelical professor of Biblical Interpretation at Eden Theological Seminary in St. Louis, who provided very helpful feedback and considerable encouragement all along the way.

chapter one

PSALMS 23 AND 22

A Profound Human Anxiety

Probably the best-known text in the Bible is Psalm 23. Numerous people can recite it whole; many more recognize its words. With a quiet, poetic promise of God's assurance and support, it has spoken to embattled lives across cultures and generations. The stories of its effect are legion. We begin with a fresh look at this treasured gem.

Psalm 23

A Psalm of David.

23 The LORD is my shepherd, I shall not want.
2   He makes me lie down in green pastures;
he leads me beside still waters;
3   he restores my soul.
He leads me in right paths
       for his name's sake.

4   Even though I walk through the darkest valley,
          I fear no evil;
for you are with me;
          your rod and your staff—
          they comfort me.

5   You prepare a table before me
          in the presence of my enemies;
you anoint my head with oil;
          my cup overflows.

6   Surely goodness and mercy shall follow me
           all the days of my life,
      and I shall dwell in the house of the Lord
          my whole life long.

The psalm uses two metaphors for God: God as a shepherd (v. 1) and God as a table host (v. 5). As a shepherd, God provides all my needs, leads me to green pastures, beside still waters, in right paths, and restores my soul. As a table host, God serves a meal, anoints my head, and overflows my cup.

A critical shift occurs in the middle of the psalm: from third person address ("he," vv. 1-3) to second person address ("you," vv. 4-5), and then back to third person ("the Lord," v. 6). Verses 4-5 are clearly the *intimate center*, a heartfelt address from me to God, a prayer instead of a description. The prayer concerns my walking through what the New Revised Standard Version (NRSV) calls "the darkest valley," what the older Revised Standard Version (RSV) called "the valley of the shadow of death." The difference is in the translation of one Hebrew term that can, in fact, be rendered either way. Bible translators swing back and forth. We shall use the RSV's more vivid "the valley of the shadow of death." The psalmist is treading a valley in which death is his close companion every step, an acutely dangerous plight. Is there a specific situation to which this psalm refers?

No certainty, but I suggest that the key word is "valley." The land of Israel is hilly and mountainous. The mountains run generally north to south and recede into flat lands only in the west near the Mediterranean coast and in the east approaching the Sea of Galilee and Jordan River. In scattered locations among all these mountains are valleys, most of them small. By far the largest and best known is the Valley of Jezreel in the north, southwest of the Sea of Galilee. Jezreel is a broad, rambling expanse with a storied history. Often, Scripture calls it simply "the valley" or "a valley," assuming that any reader will know the reference (just as any resident of the state of Virginia knows what "the valley" is).

Valleys served two main functions in the biblical era. One was to grow food. Work animals and farming implements had a much easier time on flat lands than on hillsides. Jezreel was fertile and, relative to the rest of the land, well watered with 27–30 inches of rain per year.

The other function of valleys was for fighting wars. Combat vehicles also worked much better on flat lands, and Jezreel, located on the primary northern approach into Israel, was the site of numerous military confrontations. On a hilltop overlooking Jezreel (southwest border) Israel erected the military-supply town of Megiddo, stocked with war implements and horses. The Hebrew word for "mountain" is "aram," and "aram-Megiddo" became Armageddon, the anticipated site of the great final battle between the angels of God and the forces of evil on earth. See also Ezekiel 37:1 where the valley of dry bones is clearly this same location. The Valley of Jezreel stood large in the nation's mind as a symbol of military engagement.

I suggest that "the valley of the shadow of death" refers to a battlefield, most likely Jezreel. This makes Psalm 23 the quiet prayer of a soldier preparing to go into war.

Two things, largely contradictory, happen with troops preparing for battle. One is invigoration of the macho spirit, the rev-up of a fight-mentality. War whoops, back-slapping, camaraderie shouts, a show of communal determination—football players do it on the sidelines before football games, nominating conventions before political elections, and soldiers in a pep rally before the battle. The ritual is as old as human rivalry.

Hiding beneath this show of determined spirit, however, is the subtle awareness in every troop that this could be his (or her) last engagement. "I may die here! Our opponents are strong too. The turmoil will be fierce and random, striking who-knows-where? This battle could be my last." No matter how thick the overlay of ecstatic enthusiasm, every soldier knows this deep within.

Psalm 23 speaks quietly to this inner uncertainty. "The Lord is my shepherd. . . . He restores my soul. . . . He leads me in right paths. . . ." "You are with me; your rod and staff—they comfort me": critical words of support through perilous conflict. Inside the human head, words build worlds, and a world of trust is profoundly needed. The image of God-as-my-shepherd, leading me rightly, protecting me from the hazards raging, making me strong—resonates as much in modern times as in ancient.

Troops are best sent into battle well nourished. As with modern-day competitions of many kinds, they were fed a prebattle meal. "You prepare a table before me in the presence of my enemies." (A "table" was likely a woven, roll-out mat spread across the ground.)

But the meal in Psalm 23 also gave spiritual fortification. "You anoint my head with oil" was a ritual dedication of the soldier to God.

"My cup overflows." This statement undoubtedly refers to an abundance of liquid nourishment—probably wine—provided during the meal. It also reminds me of the time I asked a friend in the state of Maine, "How did your state elections turn out?" to which he replied, "My cup runneth over!" I wonder if in ancient times, as today, the term was as much a metaphor as a reality.

In verse 6, the soldier voices confidence that the same "goodness and mercy" that will accompany him through the battle will remain with him "all the days of (his) life." He concludes with a vow that he will dwell in the house of the Lord through all his days, probably meaning that he will be devoted to God continually and faithfully.

The key moment in the psalm is verse 4, the *intimate center*: "Even though I walk through the valley of the shadow of death, I will fear no evil, for You are with me." Many of us have walked that valley, uncertain, fearful, not sure of the next step. It may have happened in military engagement or in medical struggle or in test-taking of several kinds: whenever our plight has been difficult and the dangers fierce. The word delivered by Psalm 23 is *the promise of Presence*, that we do not walk alone. A guiding, empowering Spirit walks with us. This promise of Presence, stated in the metaphor of God as shepherd, makes Psalm 23 a powerhouse of encouraging strength, the reason why it is probably the best-known text in the Bible.

A brief story.

I had a church member years ago named Frances Frazier. Frances, in her mid-fifties, lived alone in a small frame house in a paper-mill town. She had led a tragic life. Her father had died in a train accident when she was young. She had dropped out of school after the fifth grade to help support her family. Her first husband had been killed in an accident at the mill where he worked. He had jumped onto the lid of a boiler to keep hot liquid from scorching his coworkers nearby. Her second husband, after nine years, had announced that he was leaving and took most of their money with him. Yes, of course, there was another woman.

When I first met Frances, she had turned herself into a small housekeeping business and was cleaning homes. Her normal day was a sink full of dirty dishes, unmade beds, dirty bathrooms, a house full of clutter and dust, plus whatever special instructions had been left. It was all to be made perfect before the occupants came home in the afternoon.

Frances had good friends. She enjoyed going to movies or to American Legion baseball games in their small community. She showed up for almost everything happening at her church. Beneath her calm exterior was a spark of playfulness that made her both fun and interesting. Frances plodded forward, rarely looking back.

I asked her one day, "Frances, you've lived a tragic life! Far more than your share of struggle. How have you kept going, standing back up on your feet over and over?"

She looked at me earnestly and replied quite simply, "The Lord has been with me." No further explanation, no analysis. She assumed I would understand.

For a long time, I patronized that idea, thinking it a bit childlike and naïve, the product of a very simple faith. But, over years, I was told the same thing by other people who had fought through calamity and survived, "The Lord was with me."

It finally occurred one day to dumb, thick-headed me that Frances had named the most critical issue in human life: Is anyone there? Does someone else travel beside me, or am I alone?

Abandonment in a void universe is the worst human plight. Presence is the greatest gift.

After thirty-seven years as a pastor, I believe that the most pervasive mental pathology in our society is loneliness, people who feel essentially by themselves, disconnected from others. It happens among children, especially when parents devote little attention to them. With adults; the most prevalent problem that walks through the pastoral counselor's door is loneliness. It happens at all levels of the culture, having no regard for money or education.

Another brief account.

Do you remember the first question you ever asked in your life? The very first question—can you recall what it was? You were lying in your crib, perhaps three or four days old. You awoke in the night from an infant's sleep. You cried, weakly at first, then more steadily. Your cry continued until—until—someone came and picked you up and held you against her or his body, moved you about slightly, and sang softly in your ear. After a few moments, your crying stopped, because your question had been answered. What was your question? Was it not, Is anyone there? Is someone left now that I have departed the intimacy of my mother's womb? Does there remain a living being who will relate to me, an accompaniment with me? This, I suggest, was the first thing you wanted to know in your life: Is anyone there?

I stood beside the frail figure in the bed, an old man in his final days of life. He had peered up at me momentarily when I had entered the room, acknowledging with his eyes that he knew who I was. I had spoken several words, but conversation was now beyond his strength. The one thing he had done, however, was grope for my hand at his bedside. Finding it, he had gathered it into his own hands and nestled it toward his body. He closed his eyes and lay in silence. For a number of minutes I stood there, saying nothing. No word passed between us, and yet the communication was clear. "Is anyone there?" he was asking. Is there someone who is willing to travel with me through these waning moments of my life?

I am repeatedly impressed that the first question we ask in life and the last question we ask in life are exactly the same question. Our initial anxiety, and our final anxiety. And I have come to suspect that, through the many activities and pursuits that fill our lives, this remains the most critical question at all points in between.

Transport your mind now into an ancient Israelite troop encampment on the edge of the Jezreel Valley the night before a violent clash with an enemy. You, a soldier, lie in fitful sleep. You recite to yourself, "The Lord is my shepherd, I shall not want. . . ." Back at home in your village miles away, your family is also praying, but their words are Psalm 91:

> A thousand may fall at your side,
>   ten thousand at your right hand,
> but it will not come near to you. (v. 7)

> For he will command his angels concerning you
>   to guard you in all your ways. (v. 11)

Prayers for the soldier in battle emerge at several places throughout the Psalms, with Psalm 23 at the center.

Psalm 22

To the leader: according to The Deer of the Dawn. A Psalm of David.

22 My God, my God, why have you forsaken me?
>   Why are you so far from helping me, from the words of my
>   groaning?

2   O my God, I cry by day, but you do not answer;
>   and by night, but find no rest.

3   Yet you are holy,
>   enthroned on the praises of Israel.
4   In you our ancestors trusted;
>   they trusted, and you delivered them.
5   To you they cried, and were saved;
>   in you they trusted, and were not put to shame.

6   But I am a worm, and not human;
>   scorned by others, and despised by the people.
7   All who see me mock at me;
>   they make mouths at me, they shake their heads;
8   "Commit your cause to the LORD; let him deliver—
>   let him rescue the one in whom he delights!"

9   Yet it was you who took me from the womb;
>   you kept me safe on my mother's breast.
10   On you I was cast from my birth,
>   and since my mother bore me you have been my God.
11   Do not be far from me,
>   for trouble is near
>   and there is no one to help.

12   Many bulls encircle me,
>   strong bulls of Bashan surround me;
13   they open wide their mouths at me,
>   like a ravening and roaring lion.

14   I am poured out like water,
>   and all my bones are out of joint;
>   my heart is like wax;
>   it is melted within my breast;
15   my mouth is dried up like a potsherd;
>   and my tongue sticks to my jaws;
>   you lay me in the dust of death.

16   For dogs are all around me;
         a company of evildoers encircles me.
      My hands and feet have shriveled;
17   I can count all my bones,
         They stare and gloat over me;
18   they divide my clothes among themselves,
         and for my clothing they cast lots.

19   But you, O Lord, do not be far away!
         O my help, come quickly to my aid!
20   Deliver my soul from the sword,
         my life from the power of the dog!
21   Save me from the mouth of the lion!

      From the horns of the wild oxen you have rescued me.
22   I will tell of your name to my brothers and sisters;
         in the midst of the congregation I will praise you:
23   You who fear the Lord, praise him!
         All you offspring of Jacob glorify him;
         stand in awe of him, all you offspring of Israel!
24   For he did not despise or abhor
         the affliction of the afflicted;
      he did not hide his face from me,
         but heard when I cried to him.

25   From you comes my praise in the great congregation;
         my vows I will pay before those who fear him.
26   The poor shall eat and be satisfied;
         those who seek him shall praise the Lord.
         May your hearts live forever.

27   All the ends of the earth shall remember
         and turn to the Lord;
      and all the families of the nations
         shall worship before him.
28   For dominion belongs to the Lord,
         and he rules over the nations.

29   To him, indeed, shall all who sleep in the earth bow down;
         before him shall bow all who go down to the dust,
         and I shall live for him.
30   Posterity will serve him;
         future generations will be told about the Lord,
31   and proclaim his deliverance to a people yet unborn,
         saying that he has done it.

"My God, my God, why have you forsaken me?" (v. 1). This psalm begins with an absolute contradiction. "My God . . ." implies intimate, binding, unbreakable relationship, a bond not severed by any event or circumstance, similar to "my father" or "my mother" or "my child"—forever, no matter what.

"My God, my God . . ." Ancient Hebrew had no punctuation marks, including exclamation points. The way to express passion was to repeat, say it twice. "My God, my God . . ." intimacy with double exclamation! An unbreakable bond, sealed in steel!

". . . why have you forsaken me?" Abandoned me? Vanished? Consigned me to cosmic solitude? Verse 1 is a non sequitur: the first line cannot lead to the second.

Thus does Psalm 22 open by placing before us total contradiction. The Presence is absent. God has vanished. The Great Void.

Following this opening, the psalmist paints a series of metaphorical pictures depicting his/her plight.

> O my God, I cry by day, but you do not answer;
>   and by night, but find no rest. (v. 2)
>
> But I am a worm, and not human;
>   scorned by others, and despised by the people.
> All who see me mock at me;
>   they make mouths at me, they shake their heads. (vv. 6–7)
>
> Many bulls encircle me,
>   strong bulls of Bashan surround me;
> they open wide their mouths at me,
>   like a ravening and roaring lion. (vv. 12-13)

The desperation continues through the horrible scenes of verses 14-18.

These metaphorical descriptors were probably spoken originally to describe Israel's plight in the destruction of Jerusalem and the consequent exile. As they stand now, they describe the universal human experience of abandonment. The fact that someone created the psalm tells us: "It happens! It's part of the human plight! We are all susceptible! The experience can strike anyone!" The tandem of Psalms 22 and 23 is meant to speak to us when it does.

Psalm 22 goes on, in verses 19-31, to plead with God for help, for deliverance from the sword, the wild dog, and the ravenous lion. If God will help, the psalmist will preach God's deliverance in the great congregation of the faithful, will give abundant alms to the poor, will enliven many hearts, will proclaim God's saving acts to the ends of the earth—to all families of all nations, to those dead in their graves, and to future generations not yet born. This great proliferation of promise says one thing clearly: that the psalmist is desperate, but will turn to joyous and even more prolific thanksgiving if God will grant mercy.

Psalm 22 is a lament, a mournful cry for help, with bits of hope and a promise at the end. Out of the 150 psalms, lament psalms vastly outnumber all other types. They strongly dominate Books I–III (Psalms 1–89) and do not disappear in Books IV and V. It is obvious that lament—standing before God and voicing urgent plea—was a huge element in Israel's faith. To read Psalms 6–7, 10, 12–13, 17, 25–26, 31, 35, and beyond is to get the flavor.

We in the modern church have never known what to do with lament. We have based many of our hymns on psalms—the index of scriptures in any modern hymnal is filled with psalm references—but they are virtually all psalms of praise and adulation, almost never laments. Neither has lament found a place in our worship. We include a call to worship, a prayer of petition, an affirmation of faith, a Scripture reading, a sermon, an offering, and a benediction, but no opportunity for the worshiper to express struggle, upset, anger, and urgent plea. Those who come to worship deeply unsettled are told, by implication, to put a lid on it and be nice. One is not to voice the vicious words of Psalm 58, demanding that God wage vindication against the wicked. Or of Psalm 60, which chastises God for not supporting the army in battle. From some unknown place, we have concluded that in worship we are supposed to be polite to God, courteous, restrained. We are supposed to wear nice clothes, smile, and not question severely. We certainly did not get this from the Psalms.

And we pay a huge price for it. In one of my congregations' families, a teenage child committed suicide. It was—of course—deeply traumatic, horrible to the core! Church people gathered around in support, doing all the things friends do. Through those dreadful, miserable aftermath days and weeks, the church's presence and support continued.

The family's first Sunday back in worship was notable, many people greeting them with warm sympathy. Thus did things proceed. Until, a few weeks later, the family stopped coming to worship. One Sunday, two, three—no word, no explanation. I arranged to see Mom and Dad, and here is my interpretation of what they said.

"The things going on inside us right now don't belong in worship. We feel bitter, angry, abandoned, guilty, hurt. She was our beloved child; why us? This torment keeps rising in us at unexpected moments, drenching us in empty dread. We come to worship to feel uplifted, joyous, hopeful. But that's not where we are right now. We're roiling inside, and worship is not a place for that. We'll be back; that's for sure. This is our community, you are our dear friends, and you've done everything imaginable to help us. We love you. But it may take a while."

Modern worship does not offer space for lament! The ancients had an insight into us that we have lost. There will be times when we need to pray Psalm 22, to let it speak what is in our depths, to let it shout our feelings! Our neglect of this, indeed, comes with a price.

Apparently, this psalm was considered by later biblical writers to represent abandonment at its most profound. When the gospel writers, half a millennium later, described the passion of Jesus, they took Psalm 22 as their model, their table of contents. They placed "My God, my God, why have you forsaken me?" (Ps. 22:1) on Jesus' lips. They had Roman soldiers and bystanders in the crowd mock and make mouths at him (Ps 22:7). They had his mouth dry up like a potsherd and his tongue stick to his jaws (Ps 22:15). And they had the guards cast lots for his clothing (Ps 22:18). This portrays a clear picture of their esteem for Psalm 22, that it tracks a typical and authentic journey of the human soul.

Psalms 22 and 23. Psalm 22 walks us through the depths of human desolation. Psalm 23 promises that a Shepherd walks with us. Psalm 22 says that life, including the life of faith, will contain dreadful times when the path seems nothing but dark. Psalm 23 says that even with death shadowing, we need fear no evil. Psalm 22 depicts "the passion." Psalm 23 prefigures the empty tomb.

I want you to stop reading here and do an assignment. Find pen and paper. Imagine that you are writing a sermon. It is to be a one-point sermon, a single message to be delivered. That point will be:

what Psalm 23 says to Psalm 22. What the Psalms editors wanted to convey to us by placing these two documents side by side. For several years I led a section of first-year seminary students in basic preaching. Beginning preachers often suffer from fuzziness, a general idea of what they want to say but without focused clarity. I told my classes that I wanted them to begin the course with one-point sermons. They could have two or three or four sub-points under the one point, but I wanted them to be precisely certain of the main thing they wished to say. Accompanying each sermon they were to include a sentence that stated their one point. The sentence was to have no more than seven words. The sermon might be twelve to seventeen minutes long, but the defining sentence was to be short and direct. I now give you the same assignment. In no more than seven words, write down what you think Psalm 23 is saying to Psalm 22. Please don't read further until you have made a good try.

Here are what two people before you have said. "No matter how dark, light shines." Also, "Think you are alone? Look again." I, myself, have been playing with this assignment for a while, and my defining sentence is five words. "Through deepest darkness, God leads." I can visualize an entire sermon from any of these statements. What did you write?

Now, one further idea. If Psalm 23 is the prayer of a soldier going into battle, then the prebattle meal and the ritual anointing in the psalm take on intense meaning. Across the New Testament, especially in Luke's gospel and in Paul's letters, Jesus is metaphorically cast as God's holy warrior, here to battle against the sin and evil living in all human beings. As Jesus' final battle approaches, there is a preparatory meal, his "last supper" (Matt 26:26-29; Mark 14:22-25; Luke 22:14-23; 1 Cor 11:23-26). The ritual anointing is performed by a woman of Bethany (Matt 26:6-13; Mark 14:3-9; John 12:1-8) who pours an alabaster jar of costly ointment on his head. The meal and the anointing reflect Psalm 23. His passion and crucifixion echo Psalm 22.

These connections give our sacrament of Holy Communion a meaning we have not always realized. We usually think of "communion" as a time when we celebrate God's forgiveness, when bread and wine, Christ's Body and Blood, are offered to redeem us and make us new people. Hearts and souls bind with God and with one another in a renewing camaraderie.

Our analysis here suggests a second dynamic: battle preparation. When Jesus ate the Passover meal, this was nourishment for the impending conflict, a promise that even through the depths of his passion, the Lord was his Shepherd. This will mean, further, that our current-day sacrament of the Lord's Supper is also battle preparation. This may seem strange, but think further.

I remember one Sunday morning standing in the pulpit and viewing across the congregation. I knew most of them well, and I knew what they faced that afternoon or the next day. One young man supervised the loading of cargo onto airplanes. He had been told by his boss that either he would sign off on falsified loading records or he would be fired. Which was he to do, take the small risk of a jet crash, or lose his job? A woman had learned that an employee embezzled $800,000 from her business, and she was agonizing over whether there was some better alternative than sending the mother of three small children to prison. An attorney was involved in a raw, nasty courtroom battle in which the winner appeared likely to be whichever lawyer most effectively trashed the other side—not his accustomed style. A woman was a volunteer domestic relations court advocate for two children in their parents' heated and bitter divorce battle. The husband of an alcoholic wife was trying to create the best path for their oft-tortured family. These were valleys of conflict I knew about that morning, fairly normal in the everyday life of the congregation. Anyone who tries to live integrity, compassion, and faithfulness in that world is going to need an accompanying Presence. Numerous people quietly asked for it in prayer, just as that ancient soldier did. I suspect that this is why Psalm 23 is at the pinnacle of biblical passages known by believers.

Discussion Topics and Questions

1. Have you experienced Psalm 22? Do you know firsthand what this psalmist was going through? A number of different people have told stories of occasions when Psalm 23 played a strong and powerful role in their lives. Has that happened with you? When have you found yourself quietly praying it?

2. The statement, "God is with me," can also have a very destructive side. It can lead to theological arrogance, the claim that—because of my close relationship with the Almighty—my opinions, my agenda, my instructions, my orders have heightened authority. "God accompanies *me*, and *you*, therefore, should receive as truth what I say." Preachers have played this charade, presidents, corporation leaders, men with regard to women, power/authority figures of many kinds. It is usually subtle but also strong and imperialistic. Cite an example you have witnessed. If you were wanting to educate your children in how to identify the game and avoid being sucked in by the narcissistic personalities who play it, what might you try to reach them?

3. Place yourself again in that ancient army encampment the night before battle. Tomorrow there will be clash, turmoil, chaos, violence, blood, wails of pain, groaning, and death. What can you best do to calm your swirling mind on this night and get at least a little sleep?

4. Providing a time for Psalm 22-style lament in worship is a formidable challenge—I know from experience. On the one hand, we want to let worshipers express what is going on inside them, and to take every voice seriously. On the other hand, people can get consumed with upset over small neighborhood disputes and sick gerbils. Deliberate: How can a church best provide time and voice in public worship for lament? How can lament psalms be used well? If you have a poetic flair, try turning one of the lament psalms into hymn words sung to a familiar tune. Or try using a lament psalm to devise an effective responsive reading. Act as if you are on a church worship committee; try to devise an effective lament-mode to use in the congregation's worship.

5. Does the notion of the Lord's Supper as battle preparation speak to you? For some people formidable moral challenges occupy nearly every day of their lives. Can you, a person of faith, remember a struggle over fundamental integrity in which you have been involved? How might the sacrament of the Lord's Supper have strengthened your resolve?

chapter two

GENESIS 1–2 AND PSALMS 8, 19, 24, 65, 104, AND 148

The Power of the Glory

This study begins in early Genesis, the key to discerning the role of Psalms 8, 19, 24, 65, 104, and 148 in the Psalter. It is also the key to Psalm 90, which we will consider with Psalm 89 in a later chapter, and to Psalm 73, which we will consider in relation to Psalm 1. The focus of this study, God's *glory*, is a giant subject in the Psalms, often poorly discerned by our modern minds that tend to be much less attuned to it than were the ancients. Among the several critical things long-ago believers have to teach to our sophisticated, current-day minds, discernment of the *glory* ranks very high.

Genesis opens with two very different creation stories, one in 1:1–2:4a and the other in 2:4b-25. The two stories share little in common, but both are needed to present the total picture being conveyed. We will look at the second story first.

Genesis 2:4b-25

In the day that the Lord God made the earth and the heavens, [5] when no plant of the field was yet in the earth and no herb of the field had yet sprung up—for the Lord God had not yet caused it to rain upon the earth, and there was no one to till the ground; [6] but a stream would rise up from the earth, and water the whole face of the ground— [7] then the Lord God formed man from the dust of the ground, and breathed into his nostrils the breath of life; and the man became a living being. [8] And the LORD God planted a garden in Eden, in the east; and there he put the man whom he had formed. [9] Out of the ground the LORD God made to grow every tree that is pleasant to the sight and good for food, the tree of life also in the midst of the garden, and the tree of the knowledge of good and evil. [10] A river flows out of Eden to water the garden, and from there it divides and becomes four branches. [11] The name of the first is Pishon; it is the one that flows around the whole land of Havilah, where there is gold; [12] and the gold of that land is good; bdellium and onyx stone are there. [13] The name of the second river is Gihon; it is the one that flows around the whole land of Cush. [14] The name of the third river is Tigris, which flows east of Assyria. And the fourth river is the Euphrates.

15   The LORD God took the man and put him in the garden of Eden to till it and keep it. [16] And the LORD God commanded the man, "You may freely eat of every tree in the garden; [17] but of the tree of the knowledge of good and evil you shall not eat, for in the day that you eat of it you shall die."

18   Then the LORD God said, "It is not good that the man should be alone; I will make him a helper as his partner." [19] So out of the ground the LORD God formed every animal of the field and every bird of the air, and brought them to the man to see what he would call them; and whatever the man called every living creature, that was its name. [20] The man gave names to all cattle, and to the birds of the air, and to every animal of the field; but for the man there was not found a helper as his partner. [21] So the LORD God caused a deep sleep to fall upon the man, and he slept; then he took one of his ribs and closed up the place with flesh. [22] And the rib that the LORD God had taken from the man he made into a woman and brought her to the man.

[23] Then the man said,
This at last is bone of my bones
     and flesh of my flesh;
this one shall be called Woman,
     for out of Man this one was taken.
[24] Therefore a man leaves his father and mother and clings to his wife, and they become one flesh. [25] And the man and his wife were both naked, and they were not ashamed.

In this story, creation originates with an arid desert, a lifeless expanse of dry dirt. God waters the dirt and makes clay. With the clay, God—portrayed here as a potter—fashions and creates a man, Adam. God creates a garden in Eden and places the man there. In the garden, God grows trees and plants of every sort, animals of the field and birds of the air, giving Adam a lovely and welcoming home. God's ultimate gift is one of Adam's own kind, Eve. The two humans fulfill each other as does nothing else.

Soon, however (Genesis 3 and beyond), Adam and Eve, being typically human, make a fateful decision: to do things their own way, being tempted by fruit God has forbidden. This leads to their expulsion from Eden and begins a great surge of human willfulness: enmity, sexist dominance, sibling rivalry, jealousy, vengeance, arrogance, exploitation, greed, and murder. The whole biblical narrative moves forward beset by the turmoil unleashed. Story after story tells of the infection of God's Garden-of-Eden creation by human pigheadedness.

The stories after Genesis 2–3, in other words, depict how our world came to be the way we find it now. Expelled from Eden, we currently live as fugitives and wanderers on the earth, seeking to recover our lost home but never finding it. Human egos and power continually struggle against other human egos and power in violent conflicts for superiority. The saga goes forward across the millennia. This is the etiological portrait introduced by Genesis 2–3 and the chapters that follow.

Note that the creation story of Genesis 2 is very old. Both its language and its setting convey a small, primitive worldview: a garden, a water source, and a farming couple. God is close, intimate, and personal, walking the garden paths and conversing freely with the humans. The best guess is that Genesis 2 is by several hundred years the predecessor of Genesis 1, dating possibly from the tenth century BCE.

Genesis 1:1-2:4a

1   In the beginning when God created the heavens and the earth, [2] the earth was a formless void and darkness covered the face of the deep, while a wind from God swept over the face of the waters. [3] Then God said, "Let there be light"; and there was

light. ⁴ And God saw that the light was good; and God separated the light from the darkness. ⁵ God called the light Day, and the darkness he called Night. And there was evening and there was morning, the first day.

6   And God said, "Let there be a dome in the midst of the waters, and let it separate the waters from the waters." ⁷ So God made the dome and separated the waters that were under the dome from the waters that were above the dome. And it was so. ⁸ God called the dome Sky. And there was evening and there was morning, the second day.

9   And God said, "Let the waters under the sky be gathered together in one place, and let the dry land appear." And it was so. ¹⁰ God called the dry land Earth, and the waters that were gathered together he called Seas. And God saw that it was good. ¹¹ Then God said, "Let the earth put forth vegetation: plants yielding seed, and fruit trees of every kind on earth that bear fruit with the seed in it." And it was so. ¹² The earth brought forth vegetation: plants yielding seed of every kind, and trees of every kind bearing fruit with the seed in it. And God saw that it was good. ¹³ And there was evening and there was morning, the third day.

14   And God said, "Let there be lights in the dome of the sky to separate the day from the night; and let them be for signs and for seasons and for days and years, ¹⁵ and let them be lights in the dome of the sky to give light upon the earth." And it was so. ¹⁶ God made the two great lights—the greater one to rule the day and the lesser one to rule the night—and the stars. ¹⁷ God set them in the dome of the sky to give light upon the earth, ¹⁸ to rule over the day and over the night, and to separate the light from the darkness. And God saw that it was good. ¹⁹ And there was evening and there was morning, the fourth day.

20   And God said, "Let the waters bring forth swarms of living creatures, and let birds fly above the earth across the dome of the sky." ²¹ So God created the great sea monsters and every living creature that moves, of every kind, with which the waters swarm, and every winged bird of every kind. And God saw that it was good. ²² God blessed them saying, "Be fruitful and multiply and fill the waters in the seas, and let birds multiply on earth." ²³ And there was evening and there was morning, the fifth day.

24   And God said, "Let the earth bring forth living creatures of every kind: cattle and creeping things and wild animals of the earth of every kind." And it was so. [25] God made the wild animals of the earth of every kind, and everything that creeps upon the ground of every kind. And God saw that it was good.

26   The God said, "Let us make humankind in our image, according to our likeness; and let them have dominion over the fish of the sea, and over the birds of the air, and over the cattle, and over all the wild animals of the earth, and over every creeping thing that creeps upon the earth."

27   So God created humankind in his image,
    in the image of God he created them;
    male and female he created them.

[28] God blessed them, and God said to them, "Be fruitful and multiply, and fill the earth and subdue it; and have dominion over the fish of the sea and over the birds of the air and over every living thing that moves upon the earth." [29] God said, "See, I have given you every plant yielding seed that is in the face of all the earth, and every tree with seed in its fruit; you shall have them for food. [30] And to every beast of the earth, and to everything that creeps on the earth, everything that has the breath of life, I have given every green plant for food." And it was so. [31] God saw everything that he had made, and indeed, it was very good. And there was evening and there was morning, the sixth day.

2   Thus the heavens and the earth were finished, and all their multitude. [2] And on the seventh day God finished the work that he had done, and he rested on the seventh day from all the work that he had done. [3] So God blessed the seventh day and hallowed it, because on it God rested from all the work that he had done in creation.

4a   These are the generations of the heavens and the earth when they were created.

Genesis 1 is quite different from Genesis 2. It starts with a huge, dark, chaotic blob of water, a "formless deep." Creation begins with God's speaking ("And God said . . ."). With the creative power of the spoken word, God brings order into the chaos: light into the darkness, a dome (a dry space, a firmament) into the midst of the deep, land at the base of the dome, living plants and vegetation on the land, sun, moon, and stars in the heavens, fish, birds, and living creatures. God also creates two humans "in the image of God," sharing in lesser measure God's dominion over the creation. They are given God's capacity to love: "male and female he created them." The narrator of the story declares the whole of creation "good." Good, in fact, seven times over: good, good, good, good, good, good, and very good. In Hebrew, the literary repetition has enormous meaning. It depicts good beyond all measure, good to the most profound depths, genuinely, totally, and absolutely, *good*!

Whereas Genesis 2 depicts the creation of a small garden, Genesis 1 describes the creation of a grand cathedral, a sanctuary the size of the universe. The ceiling above features magnificent lights: sun, moon, and stars. The floor beneath holds vegetation and animals of every kind and fish in the waters around. The open air houses birds and other flying things.

In commentary on this scene, Psalm 19:1 says, "The heavens are telling the glory of God, and the firmament proclaims his handiwork." From every great expanse and tiny crevice, from every bold display and delicate touch, the sanctuary sings the praises of its Maker! It radiates divine majesty, announcing in loud (though silent) proclamation the *glory* of the Holy One! "When I look at your heavens, the work of your fingers, the moon and the stars which you have established . . . !" Thus does Psalm 8:3 dance with joy at viewing the Creator's work! God's *glory* rings across the universe, an eternal hymn of exultation sung to all with ears to hear the words of silence.

Genesis 1, placed at the beginning of the Bible, is an invitation *to behold*! "Look in awesome wonder!" "Take in the palace of The Holy." The chapter makes clear where faith begins: with what Abraham Joshua Heschel has called "radical amazement," the overwhelming sense of the transcendence that surrounds us, and the minuteness of our own being. Genesis 1 is an invitation to humility, to feel deep inside how tiny we are standing in God's great cathedral.

Genesis 1 was probably formulated after Jerusalem's destruction and Israel's exile (587 BCE). It reflects the expanded worldview of foreign nations and ideas. It vastly enlarges the earlier perception of God, from a local deity walking in a garden to the Architect of the universe. It moves the reader from a theology of God of our tribe or nation to the God of all tribes, nations, and worlds. From

God immanent (close to us) to, also, God transcendent (far beyond us). The theological transformation that takes place with the inclusion of Genesis 1 is enormous!

Genesis 1 also, however, plays a second role, quite vital and easily overlooked. The creation it portrays is not wrecked by the foul things humans do a bit later. Humanity goes its willful way in Genesis 3 and beyond, generating violence, bloodshed, and destruction, but the great Architect's work is unblighted. Light still shines purely, overcoming darkness. Clouds still rain fresh water. Plants grow food, despite the weeds. The sun, the moon, the stars glide unaltered in their heavenly treks. The birds fly, the fish swim, the trees dance, the hills sing, the flowers radiate magnificent beauty. Even the image-of-God-ness in people persists. Love emerges from human hearts, along with faithfulness and righteousness. The impulses to justice, forgiveness, empathy, and compassion spring forth, making us capable of profound benevolence. And, additionally, the word spoken maintains its power. Language uttered possesses enormous capacity to create new worlds.

Subsequent history, therefore, becomes the legacy not just of Genesis 2 and its corruptions but of Genesis 1 and its "good!!!" God's gift travels forward above us, beneath us, around us, and in us. It is close at hand all the time. We can behold it if we look.

Discerning eyes, however, are required. We humans can get buried beneath earth's small agendas and lose our vision of the whole. And this, as I perceive it, is a major reason why the Genesis editor placed chapter one ahead of chapter two: to declare that God's "good!!!" persists! No matter what the humans do! The beauty of God, the love of God, the creative word of God weave their way forward through history, always close by. In fact, this is history's primary reality, the larger context for all of our small squabbles. No matter how great the turmoil may seem to us, the "good!!!" gift of Genesis 1 is far greater.

Standing in awe before God's magnificence and glory can have great effect on us humans. It does not resolve our conflicts; we still must live in a badly contorted, disfigured world. But it can tell us that contortion is by no means the large picture. Awe calls us into a greater reality. I compare it with climbing through turbulent clouds in an airplane. Through the turbulence, the world is gray and dark, gusty and roiling. Our small spirits easily get buried and think that this bouncing, jostling, and sinking is everything. But, suddenly, the plane breaks through the upper layer of turbulence and we enter a brilliant blue calm, a world peaceful and good, whole again. We know, of course, that we will have to descend once more through the clouds, but they will be different. We will then be new people, because the turbulence is limited. There is a greater world surrounding. Genesis 1 is the invitation to raise our sights into the clear blue and be transformed.

The chief defining feature of Psalms 8, 19, 24, 65, 90, 104, and 148 is that they all contain footnote-type references to the great cosmic sanctuary of Genesis 1. They do not quote Genesis 1, but they refer to the "good!!!" it depicts. The Psalms and Genesis 1 both date from approximately the same era, the exile and subsequent return, and they both seem to have drawn from a common experience. I label these documents, therefore, "creation psalms." Their purpose is to draw the mind of the Psalms singer/reader to God's great creative acts, big and small.

With respect to the first five—Psalms 8, 19, 24, 65, and 90—the editors bring us toward each by nearly drowning us in vicissitude. Several lament psalms are assembled portraying the viciousness of the human plight. (Books I–III, Psalms 1–89, are rather heavily dominated by laments.) But each creation psalm injects into this darkness a glimpse of the *glory*, a vision of God's wonder. Each psalm also has a focus of its own, a subject in which it particularly is interested. But the vision of awe binds them all together.

We now consider each of the creation psalms.

Psalm 8

8   O LORD, our Sovereign,
        how majestic is your name in all the earth!

You have set your glory above the heavens.
2   Out of the mouths of babes and infants
you have founded a bulwark because of your foes,
        to silence the enemy and the avenger.

3   When I look at your heavens, the work of your fingers,
        the moon and stars that you have established;

⁴   what are humans that you are mindful of them,
         mortals that you care for them?

⁵   Yet you have made them a little lower than God,
         and crowned them with glory and honor,
⁶   You have given them dominion over the works of your hands;
         you have put all things under their feet,
⁷   all sheep and oxen,
         and also the beasts of the field,
⁸   the birds of the air, and the fish of the sea,
         whatever passes along the paths of the seas.

⁹   O LORD, our Sovereign,
         how majestic is your name in all the earth!

After the introductory Psalms 1 and 2, Psalm 3 laments over the abundance of enemies all around, praying for God's protection. Psalm 4 pleads with God to answer in distress. Psalm 5 calls for the righteousness of God against evildoers. Psalm 6 asks for recovery from an illness. Psalm 7 seeks God's help against persecutors. These laments probably come from Israel's experience in the destruction and exile. Then the editors set Psalm 8 into the sequence.

In Psalm 8, our sights are lifted to the heavens! It begins with the majesty of God proclaimed throughout the creation. God's *glory* is "above the heavens," transcending and filling the whole! Verse 2 affirms God's power over enemies, responding specifically to Psalms 3–7. Verse 3 sets before our eyes the entire universe of Genesis 1. We are invited to gaze upward into the sky and behold the *glory*, to ascend above the storm clouds and encounter the vast blue beyond!

Verse 4 states the particular focus of Psalm 8: the wondrous way God has created humans. Genesis 1:26-28 says humans were made "in the image of God." Verses 4-8 vastly expand that theme. Amid all the cosmic vastness, all the eons of time, the majestic God has chosen tiny, insignificant, fragile, temporary little you and me for exalted status. God has given us remarkable brains for thinking, remarkable language for creating, and remarkable hands for implementing, making us only "a little lower than God."

Verses 1 and 9, the identical bookends around Psalm 8, proclaim vehemently the call to amazement and wonder: "O Lord, our Sovereign, how majestic is your name in all the earth!" Come, this psalm bids, amid all your struggles with evildoers, enemies, and distress, behold the *glory*! God's great creation is still the major setting in which we live.

Psalm 9, very possibly reflecting Israel's return from exile, issues the underlying message proclaimed by Psalm 8's universe-vision.

> But the LORD sits enthroned forever,
>> he has established his throne for judgment.
> He judges the world with righteousness;
>> he judges the peoples with equity. (9:7)

God reigns! Not, finally, viciousness, not bloodshed, not destruction, not death, not the unending struggles of Psalms 3–7. God's sovereignty has not been buried beneath human sin. A glimpse of the cosmic sanctuary is the evidence!

This theme of God's reign will be vastly amplified in the latter half of the book of Psalms.

Psalm 19

19 The heavens are telling the glory of God;
       and the firmament proclaims his handiwork.
2   Day to day pours forth speech,
       and night to night declares knowledge.
3   There is no speech, nor are there words;
       their voice is not heard;
4   yet their voice goes out through all the earth,
       and their words to the end of the world.

In the heavens he has set a tent for the sun,
5   which comes out like a bridegroom from his wedding canopy,
       and like a strong man runs its course with joy.
6   Its rising is from the end of the heavens,
       and its circuit to the end of them;
       and nothing is hid from its heat.

7   The law of the LORD is perfect,
       reviving the soul;
   the decrees of the LORD are sure,
       making wise the simple;
8   the precepts of the LORD are right,
       rejoicing the heart;

the commandment of the L ORD is clear,
    enlightening the eyes;
9   the fear of the L ORD is pure,
        enduring forever;
    the ordinances of the L ORD are true,
        and righteous altogether.
10   More to be desired are they than gold,
        even much fine gold;
    sweeter also than honey,
        and drippings of the honeycomb.

11   Moreover by them is your servant warned;
        in keeping them there is great reward.
12   But who can detect their errors?
        Clear me from hidden faults.
13   Keep back your servant also from the insolent;
        do not let them have dominion over me.
    Then I shall be blameless,
        and innocent of great transgression.
14   Let the words of my mouth and the meditation of my heart
        be acceptable to you,
    O L ORD, my rock and my redeemer.

Psalms 10, 12, 13, 14, and 17 speak heartfelt lament, pleading with God for deliverance from enemies and persecutors (again, likely speaking of Israel's experience in the destruction and exile). Psalm 19 invites us back to the transcendent view.

In verses 1-2, the cosmic sanctuary—the heavens, the earth, and all creation—shouts its proclamation: "Behold, the *glory*!"

In verses 3-4, the proclamation is soundless, without an audible whisper. And yet the message is trumpeted across the entire expanse. The psalmist employs here a lovely bit of hyperbole.

Verses 4b-6 describe a morning, any and every morning: the emergence of the sun—the pinnacle of creation's light—in its daily path across the sky.

The psalm's particular focus (vv. 6-11) is God's spoken word, reflecting Genesis 1. "The law of the Lord. . . ." "The decrees of the Lord. . . ." "The precepts of the Lord. . . ." "The commandment of the Lord. . . ." "The ordinances of the Lord. . . ." The word that first formed "good!!!" across the heavenly sanctuary also creates "good!!!" in human hearts and communities. The divine proclamation that changed deep, chaotic darkness into light still invades human darkness with illumination: God's instruction!

Amid all the violence and perversion of human antics, God's spoken word is treasure, bearing the power to bring love and peace. Our waywardness has created chaotic self-serving, but God's word can make of us new people, new nations!

The psalm ends with the prayer of verses 12-14: Holy One, grant to my words the integrity of your word, the faithfulness of your word, the creativity of your word. Keep me from deceit and destructiveness, all too often the cause in which human words are used. Thus will my life be founded on a solid foundation and redeemed from its folly.

Psalm 24

24 The earth is the LORD's and all that is in it,
    the world and those who live in it;
2 for he has founded it on the seas,
    and established it on the rivers.

3 Who shall ascend the hill of the LORD?
    And who shall stand in his holy place?
4 Those who have clean hands and pure hearts,
    who do not lift up their souls to what is false,
    and do not swear deceitfully.
5 They will receive blessing from the LORD,
    and vindication from the God of their salvation.
6 Such is the company of those who seek him,
    who seek the face of the God of Jacob.

7 Lift up your heads, O gates!
    and be lifted up, O ancient doors!
    that the King of glory may come in.
8 Who is the King of glory?
    The LORD, strong and mighty,
    The LORD, mighty in battle.
9 Lift up your heads, O gates!
    and be lifted up, O ancient doors!
    that the King of glory may come in.
10 Who is the King of glory?
    The LORD of hosts,
    he is the King of glory.

After the lament in Psalm 22 and the response in Psalm 23, the editors follow with Psalm 24.

In verses 1-2, the cosmic sanctuary once again comes into view, God's authorship and ownership of the whole. Verses 3-10 are an ascent liturgy, the words of pilgrims ascending "the hill of the Lord" to worship in the Jerusalem temple.

The focus of the total psalm is to parallel the cosmic sanctuary with the earthly. The *glory* to be experienced in the great, broad creation is the same *glory* to be found in the temple of worship. As pilgrims climb Zion hill, they come not to worship a local, tribal deity but the God of all! Not simply to offer sacrifices and prayers of request to God immanent but to behold God transcendent. The heavenly sanctuary and the earthly sanctuary are one, both domiciles of the Sacred. This expands temple worship to reflect not just the local, domestic concerns of most worshipers but also to challenge them to know the universe-wide character of God. God is not just *their* God, but the God of all peoples and nations.

Thus, pilgrims are to prepare themselves devotedly! Clean hands! Pure hearts! Do not lift up your souls to what is false. Do not swear deceitfully. Thus is to be the company of "those who seek . . . the face of the God of Jacob."

The tendency of religious believers everywhere, in all times, is to domesticate God, to worship "God, our God," God of our small religious group, to the exclusion of diverse others. After the intensely personal and intimate relationship between God and believer affirmed in Psalm 23, the editors reassert here in Psalm 24 God's international character, that God is "theirs" as well as "ours," the God of ". . . the world, and (all) those who live in it" (v. 1). Within this dichotomy, between the immanent God of Genesis 2 and the transcendent God of Genesis 1, the entire biblical story moves.

Psalm 24 is a vivid reminder to every pastor and every worshiper in every age of the underlying purpose of worship: to behold the *glory*, and to stand in humble praise. The purpose of worship is not to entertain so that worshipers "enjoy it," not to attract new people into the church, not to offer psychotherapy, not to expound moralisms on how the evil world ought to behave, not to issue political commentary, not to explain theology, not to have worshipers "like the sermon," and not to raise money. The purpose of worship is to behold the *glory*, to encounter the Holy One—so that God claims us, and we know whose we are. Amid the many activities and demands in a church's life, this is treacherously easy to forget.

> Lift up your heads, O gates!
>> and be lifted up, ancient doors!
>> That the King of glory may come in. . . . (Ps 24:9)

The King of *glory*: in that Presence we stand in worship.

Psalm 65

65   Praise is due to you,
     O God, in Zion;
  and to you shall vows be performed,
2   O you who answer prayer!
  To you all flesh shall come.
3   When deeds of iniquity overwhelm us,
     you forgive our transgressions.
4   Happy are those whom you choose and bring near
     to live in your courts.
  We shall be satisfied with the goodness of your house,
     your holy temple.

5   By awesome deeds you answer us with deliverance,
     O God of our salvation;
  you are the hope of all the ends of the earth
     and of the farthest seas.
6   By your strength you established the mountains;
     you are girded with might.
7   You silence the roaring of the seas,
     the roaring of their waves,
     the tumult of the peoples.
8   Those who live at earth's farthest bounds are awed by your
     signs;
  you make the gateways of the morning and the evening shout
     for joy.

9   You visit the earth and water it,
     you greatly enrich it;
  the river of God is full of water;
     you provide the people with grain,
     for so you have prepared it.

10   You water its furrows abundantly,
        settling its ridges,
    softening it with showers,
        and blessing its growth.
11   You crown the year with your bounty;
        your wagon tracks overflow with richness.
12   The pastures of the wilderness overflow,
        the hills gird themselves with joy,
13   the meadows clothe themselves with flocks,
        the valleys deck themselves with grain,
        they shout and sing together for joy.

Psalms 52–64 play with various angles of the theme of protection against enemies. The foes proliferate, and pleas to God fill these psalms. In Psalms 69–71, prayers for deliverance from adversaries resume. Placed in this harsh sequence is Psalm 65, a psalm of harvest thanksgiving to be sung in temple worship.

Verses 1-4 form the introduction, declaring praise to God and blessing upon those who gather.

Verses 5-8 return us to Genesis 1, speaking of God's great power, in establishing the mountains and girding them with might, in silencing the roaring seas, and in stilling "the tumult of the peoples." To the farthest ends of the earth humanity is "awed by your signs," by the magnificence of the creation. Every morning and every evening shout with joy the wondrous power of God.

The particular focus of this psalm is a series of mundane occurrences, things that happen right here, right now, close by, in our midst: rain that enriches the earth, grain that grows from the soil, bounty that spreads richness across the land, hills girded in joy, meadows clothed with flocks, and valleys decked in grain. To those with eyes to see, the wonder of God's creative might radiates from the whole, broadcasting the praise of the Maker. The holy sanctuary resides not only in the heavens and in the temple but also in the fields, in falling rain, in nurturing dirt, in germinating seeds, in food for eating, in the beauty of flowers and plants, in animals that graze, in mountains that rejoice. When the human heart recognizes this, it will live continuously in God's sacred places with unending awe and praise!

The main relationship most of us have with rain is to complain when it gets us wet. Our main relationship with dirt is that it must be wiped off our shoes when we come indoors. Our main relationship with fruits, vegetables, grains, and meats is that we presume their ready availability in the grocery store. Rarely or never do we behold hills girding themselves with joy or pastures, meadows, and valleys shouting and singing together. We do celebrate a year crowned with bounty, thawing a frozen bird and gathering with family to overindulge. Shortly thereafter, however, many of us throw ourselves into the shopping orgy of Black Friday. Psalm 65 is an invitation to behold a world very close by to which we are often blind, a world that is free with no tickets necessary, the world of God's ongoing creative miracle. This psalm suggests that small farmers, those daily and directly connected with fields, produce, and living animals, may have some profound theological lessons to teach to the rest of us. Urban and most suburban life is incredibly insulating from the fundamental sources of our well-being. I wonder what a theological seminar on this subject would look like.

Psalm 104

Psalm 104 is the most extensive creation story in the Bible. It is placed between a psalm of thanksgiving for God's forgiveness (Psalm 103) and a psalm of God's faithfulness (Psalm 105). We are now in Book IV of Psalms, having moved through and beyond the great concentration of laments in Books I–III. Books IV–V look forward toward God's relationship with the future Israel, after the exile and the return.

Psalm 104 starts and ends (almost) with the formula, "Bless the Lord, O my soul," bookends around the whole. This makes clear what Genesis 1 never says specifically: that the purpose of the creation account is to evoke praise, honor, awe, and wonder in those who sing it. "May the glory of the Lord endure forever. . .": verse 31, states the psalm's message.

Psalm 104 bids us early to behold the Magnificence.

> You are clothed with honor and majesty
>   wrapped in light as with a garment. (vv. 1b-2a)

> You make the clouds your chariot,
>   you ride on the wings of the wind. (v. 3b)

But it quickly moves to an extended description of the creation's splendor.

> You stretch out the heavens like a tent. (v. 2b)

> You set the earth on its foundations,
>   so that it shall never be shaken. (v. 5)

> You make springs gush forth in the valleys,
>   they flow between the hills,
> giving drink to every wild animal;
>   the wild asses quench their thirst.
> By the streams the birds of the air have their habitation;
>   they sing among the branches. (vv. 10-12)

Through these middle verses, Psalm 104 exhilarates in how God provides on earth for the needs of the huge variety of living things: wild animals, donkeys, birds, grass, cattle, plants, and people.

> You cause the grass to grow for the cattle,
>   and plants for people to use,
> to bring forth food from the earth,
>   and wine to gladden the human heart,
> oil to make the face shine,
>   and bread to strengthen the human heart.
> The trees of the LORD are watered abundantly,
>   the cedars of Lebanon that he planted.
> In them the birds build their nests;
>   the stork has its home in the fir trees.
> The high mountains are for the wild goats,
>   the rocks are a refuge for the coneys. (vv. 14-18)

> You have made the moon to mark the seasons;
>   the sun knows its time for setting. (v. 19)

> People go out to their work
>   and to their labor until the evening. (v. 23)

The litany over God's creation proceeds, describing mainly the great harmony built into the cosmos, the beautiful resonance across the creation. Each portion serves its needed role among the rest. Psalm 104 is Genesis 1 in the present tense. According to this psalm, Genesis 1 did not just happen back then but continues now, an on-flowing reality close by.

Death is pictured as an entirely natural part of life, a portion of what happens to beings surrounded by the Creator's love. And so is renewal:

> When you hide your face, they are dismayed;
>> when you take away their breath, they die
>> and return to their dust.
> When you send forth your spirit, they are created;
>> and you renew the face of the ground. (vv. 29-30)

The psalm ends in praise and wonder, with the final request that God remove human sin and wickedness from the great accord (v. 35a).

Psalm 104 is a portrait of "good!!!"—now! It acknowledges evil (v. 35), but it envelops it as a tiny reality within creation's great vista. This psalm, as a result, defines faith, the conviction that—no matter how deep our darkness—there is a great light not diminished. That "the sufferings of this present time are not even worth comparing with the glory that is to be revealed" (Rom 8:18). That traveling with us, beyond us, and in us is God's creation-gift. Psalm 104 is the new Genesis 1 for postexilic Israel, a vision of our fundamental circumstance. I suggest that, to those mired in the struggle, it is also a vision of what *will be*, of where God's power and love intend to take us. Genesis 1 and Psalm 104 alike are not presented to us so much as history but as destination. They are portraits of the promise. Revelation 21 and 22 might well have been fashioned around their vision.

Psalm 148

148 Praise the LORD!
>> Praise the LORD from the heavens;
>>> praise him in the heights.
² Praise him, all his angels;
>> praise him, all his host!

3   Praise him, sun and moon;
        praise him, all you shining stars!
4   Praise him, you highest heavens,
        and you waters above the heavens!

5   Let them praise the name of the LORD,
        for he commanded and they were created.
6   He established them forever and ever;
        he fixed their bounds which cannot be passed.

7   Praise the LORD from the earth,
        you sea monsters and all deeps,
8   fire and hail, snow and frost,
        stormy wind fulfilling his command!

9   Mountains and all hills,
        fruit trees and all cedars!
10 Wild animals and all cattle,
        creeping things and flying birds!
11 Kings of the earth and all peoples,
        princes and all rulers of the earth!
12 Young men and women alike,
        old and young together!

13 Let them praise the name of the LORD,
        for his name alone is exalted;
        his glory is above earth and heaven.
14 He has raised up a horn for his people,
        praise for all his faithful,
        for the people of Israel who are close to him.
    Praise the LORD!

Here, in Psalm 148, is the Psalms editors' final glimpse of the accompanying *glory*. No longer are we surrounded by psalms of hardship and lament but now by praise and joy. God has, at the beginning of Book V (Psalm 107) sent forth God's powerful stead-fast love into every embattled human circumstance and gathered the scattered faithful (more on this later). The virtues of God's in-struction, God's commandments, in ordering the life of the renewed nation and its people are lauded (Psalm 119). Hymns of ascent once again can be heard on the pilgrimage pathways up to Mount Zion (Psalms 120–134). We can proclaim that no matter how far we are driven from home, into exile, to the heights of heaven, to the depths of Sheol, we find God's presence with us (Psalm 139), God's stead-fast love seeking to reclaim us (Psalm 107). And, as the book of Psalms moves toward its conclusion with six hymns of uninter-rupted praise (Psalms 145–150), the editors inject a final glimpse of the *glory* that has accompanied us throughout. Psalm 148 pro-vides the cosmic dimension in this six-psalm sequence.

It sings praise from the first word! It calls on all elements in the created order—heights, depths, angels, hosts, sun, moon, stars, wa-ters, sea monsters, fire, hail, snow, frost, stormy wind, mountains, hills, fruit trees, cedars, animals, cattle, creeping things, flying birds, kings, princes, rulers, young men, young women, old, young—the whole Genesis 1 universe, to join in one magnificent chorus. We can hear the music filling the heavens, the great proclamation broadcast throughout the earth. Every created being lends its voice: "Praise to God! Praise to God!"

I remember feeling particularly a part of that chorus. The city where I attended college (Raleigh, NC) sponsored each year a community-wide *Messiah* sing. From the interior of the bass section, I joined perhaps 120 other voices plus soloists and orchestra. We started in the wilderness ("Comfort, comfort ye, my people") and worked through the struggles and vicissitudes of human life. "The Hallelujah Chorus" resounded, but the greatest moment came at the end: "Worthy Is the Lamb," in which "blessing and honor and glory and power be unto him, be unto him!" was repeated time after time after time in a crescendo of declaration. And the whole concluded with the "Amen" chorus, reaching unrivaled heights of artistic exclamation. In those moments, George Frederick Handel (God, indeed, works through unlikely earthen vessels!) transcended the confines of the Raleigh auditorium and connected us with the universe, pouring out praise across the whole! This is the scene Psalm 148 portrays. We are bidden to join every living creature in extolling the God of creation! With that, the book of Psalms ends.

Synthesis

Psalms 8, 19, 24, 65, 104, and 148 (and, as we shall see, Psalms 90 and 73) join one another in beckoning us to *behold*! Behold the *glory* across God's creation. Behold the radiance of God's universe.

Behold the power, the wonder, the love. These psalms issue to the five books of Psalms the same invitation Genesis 1 offers to the five books of the Torah: to raise our gaze beyond earth's chaos and sight the larger realm. The *glory* is still present: above us, beneath us, around us, and within us each day and night, and we are invited into the sacred act of perceiving it in awe.

Awe can transform us. Instill in us profound regard for human life, the image-of-God-ness in each one (Psalm 8). It can beckon us to honor language, one of God's most sacred gifts, in a world where carefully crafted language deception has become a high-paying occupation (Psalm 19). It can re-tune us to the underlying purpose of worship, reminding us that this is for all humanity, not just our tribe and nation (Psalm 24). It can alert us that, buried in the most mundane items of every day—rain, dirt, seeds, grain, pastures, flocks—God's creative hand is fully visible (Psalm 65). It can overwhelm us, proclaiming that, built into the entire natural order, is a sacred harmony that provides magnificently for earth's living beings (Psalm 104). It can invite us to the great symphony performed by the entire creation, a performance of praise and exultation (Psalm 148). Awe before the *glory*! It can deliver to us the critical insight that the embattled world of our struggles is in reality quite small compared with the totality of God's gift. And that despite our human rebelliousness, the heart of love residing at the center of the universe has not diminished. The Psalms editors wanted to convey this message with conviction and certainty!

Discussion Topics and Questions

1. Recall from your life an experience of profound awe, a moment of wonder and astonishment. What caused it? What did it cause in you? How were you different afterward? Is awe frequent in your life or rare? How might you best open yourself to experience more? By slowing down and noticing things around you? By listening more intently? By reflecting on things that happen? By spending more quiet time outdoors? By higher-quality conversation with other people?

2. In an article in the May 24, 2015 *New York Times*, "Why Do We Experience Awe?" Dr. Paul Piff and Dr. Dacher Keltner, professors of psychology, cast a further perspective on awe, indicating that it is "the ultimate 'collective' emotion," motivating people "to do things that enhance the greater good. . . ." They suggest that people who regularly feel wonder and beauty in the world around them tend to create stronger groups and more cohesive communities, to be more generous to the stranger, less narcissistic and entitled. They believe that our culture today is "awe-deprived," producing people who are "more individualistic, more self-focused, more materialistic, and less connected to others."

What do you make of their research conclusions? Of the concept of awe-deprivation? Have you had experiences in which awe enhanced camaraderie, community?

3. Author Anthony Doerr recently published a novel entitled *All the Light We Cannot See*. Set in World War II, it depicts the horrors of war, not only the physical destruction but how war steals the fundamental humanity of humans, turning us into wild beasts. Cruelty abounds: across the battle lines, within the ranks—no one is spared the tortures waged by imperialistic egos granted sanction and power. Repeatedly through the story, however, the moon shines, the stars gleam, the ocean rolls, the birds fly, the winds rustle, and human hearts reach forth in astounding acts of empathy and self-sacrifice. Even the fiercest human figure in the book toward the end performs a decisive act of compassion. The war ends with destruction and death all around, a massive scene of earth-chaos. But, time moves forward beyond the war, and beauty re-emerges, larger and more lasting than the chaos. The light was there throughout, but for months and years deep darkness hid it from human eyes. Only one person in the story could see it throughout, a young woman who was blind.

Not once throughout the book does author Doerr speak the name of God or mention the Bible, but his story is a poignant modern version of the Psalms editors' point. Anthony Doerr won a Pulitzer Prize for his book. Do you find it a realistic portrait of life, or is it sentimental dreaming? Is life at base a destructive, pitiless, hopeless jungle? Should Genesis 1 never have been set at the front of the Bible? Or is there, in fact, at the center of our universe a heart of love?

4. The Psalms are poems. Poetry bears a special character. Prose uses words to speak what we understand; poetry uses words to speak what is beyond our understanding. Prose delivers information; poetry paints pictures. Prose expounds the rational. Poetry bids us to set aside the rational and enter the world of feelings, passions, heartaches, joy, longing, beauty, and love. Prose is the language of knowledge. Poetry is the language of imagination and awe. Might it be that the editors' major purpose throughout the Psalms is not at all to deliver information but to evoke wonder, to carry us into the presence of the Holy One, from which comes wisdom, compassion, and purpose?

5. I ask you to do something. Take at least fifteen minutes, preferably thirty. If you get addicted, keep going.

Pick a clear night. Lie on your back under the sky. Gaze upward. Soak in the cosmic sanctuary, the vastness, the brilliance, the beauty. Think about how often this spectacle is available to you and how seldom you make use of it. Think of ancient Hebrew shepherds who spent most of their nights under this same sky without surrounding electric lights to dim their view. Realize that some of the starlight you are seeing originated before human beings took their first step on this planet two hundred thousand years ago. Ponder the notion that beyond the stars you see are millions and millions and millions more you cannot see. Consider that you and I have no idea what is beyond the outer extremities or where our grand universe is headed in its journey. Think of the absurdity of our believing that we, tiny, temporary humans, "own" pieces of this earth, holding title. Meditate on Leviticus 25:23, "The land shall not be sold in perpetuity, for the land is mine; you are but aliens and tenants." Think of the scene as God's artistic studio, where beauty originated, and ask what role God needs you to play in this design.

Or—gaze at a newborn child. Behold tiny fingers, hands, nose, mouth. Realize that just a short time ago this was one cell joining another, and ask how so perfect an elaboration could come from such simplicity. Wonder what guiding power has made right arm and left arm, right leg and left leg, essentially mirror images in marvelous coordination, and will now cause them to grow in like form. Wonder at the millions of electrical connections in that small head necessary for this tiny bundle to become a strong adolescent, playing sports or musical instruments, reading books, and learning new universes. Ponder how caressing and cuddling this helpless mite can be so primally fulfilling to mother, father, child, and others.

Or—gaze into a blossomed mountain laurel flower and note the delicacy of color and shape, masterfully engineered to attract bees and exchange pollen.

Or—watch the sun rise over a mountain scape, slowly lowering light into a valley, with changing colors and designs.

Or—gaze at creek water flowing over stones, and see if you can identify what is so soothing about the gentle sound. Think of the number of years the scene before you has been happening. Think of the natural beauty you are looking at. Think of the huge number of little worlds—of crawling things and flying bugs, of green plants, of tiny water creatures, of birds, of fish, of amphibians—that reside in the space you are observing.

Or—lie very still in some quiet place and listen to the third movement of Beethoven's ninth symphony. Wonder how simple tunes can be so beautiful, and how they can be woven together intricately to create gorgeous designs. Wonder how a deaf man could concoct a musical sound this appealing to the ears and minds of millions of people afterward.

Or—write the story of some personal event that deeply touched your heart. A psychologist friend of mine has said, "When people tell one another their stories, the Sacred enters the room." Story brings forth the true contours of the worlds that live in us.

Or—recall and ponder words spoken to you that have made a tremendous creative difference in your life. Think about what has resulted from those words, their creativity. Think of how differently things might have gone without them.

Now, in a short paragraph or a poem, describe what your mind and soul experienced as you engaged in the activity you chose. Would you benefit from having the experience more often? How might you make that happen?

chapter three
PSALMS 1 AND 73

Transcending the Great Moral Enigma

What happens between these two psalms relates directly to the "creation psalms" just considered. It also relates to the lives you and I are living at this very day and hour.

Psalm 1

1   Happy are those
      who do not follow the advice of the wicked,
   or take the path that sinners tread,
      or sit in the seat of scoffers;
2   but their delight is in the law of the LORD,
      and on his law they meditate day and night.
3   They are like trees
      planted by streams of water,
   which yield their fruit in its season,
      and their leaves do not wither.
   In all that they do, they prosper.

4   The wicked are not so,
      but are like chaff that the wind drives away.
5   Therefore the wicked will not stand in the judgment,
      nor sinners in the congregation of the righteous;
6   for the LORD watches over the righteous,
      but the way of the wicked will perish.

Psalm 1 presents in beautiful, simple verse a moral formula depicting the world as God created it: the righteous will prosper; the wicked will suffer. Those who delight in God's instruction (law), who meditate on it day and night, who avoid the path of sinners, are like well-watered trees that grow strong, bear abundant fruit in season, and live long lives. Those who do evil and sit in the seat of scoffers are like chaff blown aloft and carried away by the wind, disintegrating into nothing. Lead a good life and you will be rewarded with strength and endurance; lead a wicked life and you will be cast away to empty obscurity. Psalm 1 sets down its clear moral formula.

The Psalms editors anchor the book with this formula. It is the foundation on which all the rest is built. To believe it and to live it is to be a faithful human being, a righteous community. This instruction stands at the center of life!

The editors did not create the formula. It was the dominant theology of their time. It came from the "Mosaic" or "Deuteronomic" understanding of God's covenant with Israel. The book of Deuteronomy expounds it extensively. After twenty-nine chapters of instruction spoken by God through Moses on how to conduct the community's life, Deuteronomy exhorts:

> See, I have set before you today life and prosperity, death and adversity. If you obey the commandments of the LORD . . . , then you shall live and become numerous, and the LORD your God will bless you. . . . But if your heart turns away and you do not hear. . ., you shall perish. . . . I have set before you life and death, blessings and curses. Choose life so that you and your descendants may live . . . (30:15-20).

If God's former covenant, guaranteeing the eternity of the Davidic line of kings, had been severely wounded by the destruction of Jerusalem (see chapter four that follows), God's new covenant would be a covenant of God's law written on human hearts. It would be a call to rigor, to a new pledge of religious devotion. Psalm 1 is a statement of that call.

But, subsequent to Psalm 1, the Psalms editors move us through a long procession of documents that show how fragile the formula is and even question whether it is true. Psalm after psalm depicts life situations that question Psalm 1. How can evil fare handsomely while goodness and righteousness are tormented? the lament psalms of Books I–III ask. These psalms also question repeatedly how long God will put up with it. Where is God while deceitful merchants swindle the poor and profit royally, while the wealthy buy favorable judgments in the courtroom, while partying socialites disregard the widows and orphans struggling to survive just outside their gates, while the powerful steal from the weak, and while armies from arrogant, wicked nations defeat our own? Psalm laments are not simply over the rotten state of things but over how this rottenness can happen if Psalm 1 is true.

Psalm 73

73 Truly God is good to the upright,
    to those who are pure in heart.
2 But as for me, my feet had almost stumbled;
    my steps nearly slipped.
3 For I was envious of the arrogant;
    I saw the prosperity of the wicked.

4 For they have no pain;
    their bodies are sound and sleek.
5 They are not in trouble as others are;
    they are not plagued like other people.
6 Therefore pride is their necklace;
    violence covers them like a garment.
7 Their eyes swell out with fatness;
    their hearts overflow with follies.
8 They scoff and speak with malice;
    loftily they threaten oppression.
9 They set their mouths against heaven,
    and their tongues range over the earth.

10 Therefore the people turn and praise them,
    and find no fault in them.
11 And they say, "How can God know?
    Is there knowledge in the Most High?"
12 Such are the wicked;
    always at ease, they increase in riches.

13   All in vain I have kept my heart clean
        and washed my hands in innocence.
14   For all day long I have been plagued,
        and am punished every morning.

15   If I had said, "I will talk on in this way,"
        I would have been untrue to the circle of your children.
16   But when I thought how to understand this,
        it seemed to me a wearisome task,
17   until I went into the sanctuary of God;
        then I perceived their end.
18   Truly you set them in slippery places;
        you make them fall to ruin.
19   How they are destroyed in a moment,
        swept away utterly by terrors!
20   They are like a dream when one awakes;
        on awaking you despise their phantoms.

21   When my soul was embittered,
        when I was pricked in heart,
22   I was stupid and ignorant;
        I was like a brute beast toward you.
23   Nevertheless I am continually with you;
        you hold my right hand.
24   You guide me with your counsel,
        and afterward you will receive me with honor.
25   Whom have I in heaven but you?
        And there is nothing on earth that I desire more than you.
26   My flesh and my heart may fail,
        but God is the strength of my heart and my portion forever.

27   Indeed, those who are far from you will perish;
        you put an end to those who are false to you.
28   But for me it is good to be near God;
        I have made the LORD God my refuge,
        to tell of all your works.

Psalm 73 gathers the moral enigma into a single, crisp statement.
It opens by issuing full acknowledgment of Psalm 1:

    Truly God is good to the upright,
        to those who are pure in heart. (v. 1)

But it then turns to question the assertion:

> . . . as for me, my feet had almost stumbled;
> my steps had nearly slipped.
> For I was envious of the arrogant;
> I saw the prosperity of the wicked. (vv. 2-3)

I nearly lost my moral bearings when I looked at life around me and realized how richly wickedness is sometimes rewarded! Evil can reap enormous prosperity for those who practice it craftily!

The psalm then moves through a litany (vv. 4-12) of the violent, conscienceless, shameless, arrogant ways of the wicked: "pride is their necklace; violence covers them. . . ," "they scoff and . . . threaten." Not only do they exploit their fellow humans but they scoff at God, declaring that their wickedness has no consequence. And, further—worst of all—they are praised by the people, lauded as outstanding and virtuous, lifted to the heights of human glory! No one pays attention to the deep, corrosive fault at their core, only to their success! They are not tormented by the evil of their ways; they simply keep getting more wealthy!

The psalmist agonizes deeply over this contradiction!

> All in vain I have kept my heart clean
> and washed my hands in innocence. (v. 13)

I have sought diligently to lead a good life, to follow Psalm 1, but my efforts have taken me nowhere.

> For all day long I have been plagued,
> and am punished every morning. (v. 14)

The prosperity of the wicked torments me! I awake to it each new day.

> If I had said, "I will talk on in this way,"
> I would have been untrue to the circle of your children. (v. 15)

Here is a key verse in interpreting the psalm. The psalmist, it turns out, is a teacher, one who instructs younger people. "The circle of your children" is his class. The issue is: What is he to teach them? Is he to teach Psalm 1, that they should devote their lives to integrity? Or should he teach actual life as he sees it around him: learn to do evil with craft and guile, and therefore prosper?

I could not urge them to evil, he says. This would have been to forsake the trust placed in me as their teacher.

> But when I thought how to understand this,
> it seemed to me a wearisome task . . . (v. 16)

Sometimes the New Revised Standard Version of the Bible absolutely excels in understatement, and this is one of those moments. "It seemed to me a wearisome task," indeed! Try instead, "It was torment at the foundation of my soul!" "It gnawed fiercely in my gut!" "Day and night it plagued me!" Samuel Terrien translates the verse, "It was only misery in my eyes" (*The Psalms, Strophic Structure and Theological Commentary* [Grand Rapids, MI: Eerdmans, 2003], 524).

> . . . until I went into the sanctuary of God;
> then I perceived their end. (v. 17)

Again, Terrien: "Until I came to the sacred places of God" (the Hebrew word translated "sanctuary" is, in fact, a plural). Until I stood on holy ground and beheld the *glory*! Until the cosmic portrait of Genesis 1 appeared before me as a marvelous and breathtaking reality! Until the purity of God's light cast its beams into my face. Then I *knew* what I *must do*, who I must be. My indecision vanished. No, the moral enigma did not resolve. Evil still prospered. But this no longer tormented me, dominated me. The great moral enigma was transcended. The greatest dilemmas of our existence are often not resolved, but they may be transcended.

Verses 18-20 clarify where evil finally leads: to ruin. This, of course, not according to the factual data of daily life but according to Psalm 1, to the faith of the psalmist.

I turned away from you! I was tempted to sever our relationship! I turned dumb and stupid (vv. 21-22). But, having beheld your majesty,

> Nevertheless I am continually with you;
>> you hold my right hand.
> You guide me with your counsel,
>> and afterward you will receive me with honor. (vv. 23-24)

Verses 27-28 provide a final flourish.

It is verse 17 that depicts a critical moment in the life of faith: entering "the sanctuary" and beholding the *glory*. "The sanctuary," "the sacred places of God," may be a building made by human hands atop Zion hill. It may be the Washington Cathedral or any of the thousands of smaller versions. It may be the great sanctuary of the magnificent heavens that unfolds itself before our vision in a dark-night sky. It may be the serenity of a flowing brook with its soft, gentle sounds and eternal constancy. It may be any of the wonders alluded to in the creation psalms of the previous chapter. Whatever evokes in us holy awe, that is "the sanctuary."

Beholding the *glory* certainly does not fix the problem, but it does invite the beholder into transformation. I cannot willingly live evil in God's holy place. I cannot stand in the Divine Presence knowing myself a fraud and a cheat. I will pursue integrity. Beholding God's *glory* settles the issue.

Psalm 73:17 is a key moment in the Psalter, perhaps the central pivot in the entire drama. (A similar moment occurs when Psalm 89 transitions to Psalm 90; see chapter 4.) All before has been plagued by enigma: "Why does wickedness prosper, and how do I keep from being lured into it?" Soon after Psalm 73, the Psalms will move toward undiluted singing and joy before the *glory*. This, to the Psalms editors, is awe's effect.

The desire to be good, honest people, oriented to integrity, resides in most of us. We commonly say, "I want to be able to sleep at night," meaning that we don't want tortured consciences. The impulse to do what is good seems part of our innate human makeup. It is hopefully encouraged by parents and family, often by neighborhood and community; also by the legal punishments for wrongdoing. Religion nourishes it, also hopefully school. The question posed by Psalm 73 is: How do we bring forward this inner desire when we face strong temptation to violate it, when wrong promises a result we very much want? Four examples.

I worked for seven years as a pastor in a low-, low-income neighborhood, the former labor village of a large cigarette manufacturing company. I witnessed in that neighborhood an all-too-common event. As teenagers finished their secondary schooling and moved toward adulthood, ages 17 and 18, they faced two dominant work choices. One was to take what was called an "entry-level job" at McDonald's or Arby's or Burger King, labor through fast-food hours in a hot kitchen, and earn $250 per week. The other was to deal junk, selling undercover and earning $1,500 to $2,000 per week. Most never considered the second alternative because they knew they did not want to live that kind of life. A few did and were sucked into crime. It was tempting!

A farmer in middle Kentucky once took me on a tour of his farm, along a dirt road with fields on both sides. Midway along, he stopped. "Look to your right," he said. "In those fields I am growing produce: beans, corn, squash, tomatoes, kale, collards, eggplant. I will earn $650 per acre. Now look to your left. In those fields I am growing tobacco for use in making cigarettes. There, I will earn $2,200 per acre. Given a tough, competitive market and a growing family, tell me what I should do."

In the May 2015 issue of *The Atlantic* was an article asking whether bankers can be good. The article described efforts within the banking industry to encourage integrity, but also a large temptation not to. Banking, the article said, moves in two directions. One is toward community and personal service, in which the bank's purpose is to provide dependable, high-quality money management, loan, and investment services to community clients. This was the original purpose of banks, and it depends heavily on honesty, faithfulness, and good reputation. The bank makes money but not in huge sums. The service plays a major role in strengthening the community and its people. The other direction banking can take is toward bundling large packages of assets—loans, bonds, or whatever—and selling them as investments to other banks or institutions. The most clever and luckiest bankers at bundling make huge earnings, are rewarded with high salaries, and are promoted to the top. These are the people who really "succeed," based not on integrity but on wit and sometimes guile. Their big gains, however, are someone else's big losses. It is bank against bank to see who can outplay whom. Can the industry control itself and behave?—this was the article's question. The banking industry is having a very difficult time even asking that question of itself, much less answering it, the article said.

Political campaigns, especially big ones, have become vexing drudgery for most Americans. Trash upon trash upon trash we have to endure, candidates throwing wild charges at one another in an orgy of self-righteous accusation whose purpose is to make voters vote according to their resentment and anger. An American presidential campaign makes many of us want to withdraw from society until it is over. Why do the candidates turn to slime? *Because it works!* Framing your opponent as a dishonest, ugly, unreliable cheat catches voter attention and wins votes—much more effectively than setting forth one's own positions and qualifications. There are very profitable businesses today that will sell to any candidate of any persuasion their well-honed abilities at trashing an opponent. The total process produces divisive government, unable to lead the nation forward in directions the nation needs to go. Evil prospers because we vote for it!

Discussion Topics and Questions

1. Psalm 1 contrasts "the righteous" with "the wicked." In our modern vocabulary, "righteous" is often not a flattering word, mainly because of its association with the concept "self-righteous." We think of holier-than-thou. But in ancient Hebrew (including Psalm 1), "righteous" meant being a high-quality person and seeking what is right, but, well beyond that, it meant devoting your life to the good of your community, living for the whole, wanting genuinely to improve your people's destiny—what we in our time call "statesmanship." The Hebrew tradition celebrates such lives, giving thanks for the vital role they play. Being a virtuous person is honorable, but being a righteous person is outstanding! Among people you know of, describe someone you would name as righteous.

2. If you were a teenager in that low-income labor village deciding what to do in your life after high school, or that mid-Kentucky

farmer deciding what to grow in your fields, what factors would weigh heaviest in your decision?

3. If you were a young, talented, competitive business school graduate looking to build a successful career and a stock portfolio as a banker, what would constrain you from using your full savvy and even guile to package mortgages to sell to other institutions, especially when you knew that everybody else was doing it, that this was widely understood as "the way the game is played these days?"

4. In my experience, many folks continue to suspect, deep inside, that poor people are poor because they are lazy, devious, and immoral, not to be trusted. A great many others believe that successful, wealthy people are thereby virtuous, to be honored and emulated by others. Have you experienced these attitudes in your world? In yourself?

5. Describe a time when you were tempted to win by doing evil. Was there something that kept you from it? Did you, by chance, grow up with a natural, internal wall against such behavior?

6. Has there been a time when the rigor of Psalm 1—the psalm presents a rigorous challenge—has laid heavily upon you, when you have felt compelled to do a superior job at some task?

chapter four

PSALMS 89 AND 90

A Profound Search for Light

Psalm 89, which marks the end of Book III of the Psalter, is a deeply heartrending lament over the destruction of Jerusalem and the failure of God's covenant with King David. Psalm 90, which begins Book IV, is the Psalms editors' response to this trauma, a "creation psalm." To get the picture, we need background.

The Davidic Covenant

Second Samuel 7 is pivotal in Israel's history. The story told comes from around 985 BCE. Israel was a very young nation, having anointed its first monarch, King Saul, around 1020–1015 BCE, and then King David, in 1000 BCE. The monarchy had been created primarily to resist military invasions into Israel's territory by hostile neighbors—the Midianites, the Philistines, and others—and the young David had succeeded quite well! He had built a strong Israelite fighting force, had waged a series of victorious military campaigns against the warring neighbors, and had brought a time of relative peace and well-being to his own nation.

David's chief "court prophet," Nathan, came to David one day with rather incredible news from God. Kings in that time regularly maintained court prophets whose job was to deliver messages from the Divine concerning the king's rule. Nathan's report is found in 2 Samuel 7:1-17.

God was making a covenant with David, Nathan said, a firm commitment guaranteed forever, through all generations. The word "forever" is used three times in the story to underline the divine certainty. Under the covenant, God promised to make for David "a great name, like the name of the great ones of the earth" (v. 9). That is, King David would become renowned far and wide, throughout all times. "And I will appoint a place for my people Israel and will plant them, so that they may live in their own place, and be disturbed no more; and evildoers shall afflict them no more, as formerly" (v. 10). ". . . the LORD will make you a house. . . . I will raise up your offspring after you, who shall come forth from your body, and I will establish his kingdom. He shall build a house for my name, and I will establish the throne of his kingdom forever. I will be a father to him, and he shall be a son to me. . . . I will not take my steadfast love from him. . . . Your house and your kingdom shall be made sure forever before me, your throne shall be established forever" (vv. 12-16).

God was promising, in short, that Jerusalem would be protected from all violent intruders, and that the Davidic line of kings would remain secure on Israel's throne—all of it forever. Guaranteed by God's *steadfast love*, a love that was the essence of God's being. God's steadfast love was a strong, powerful force that no earthly power could overthrow. God's steadfast love encircled the Holy City as a protective wall, and it maintained the sons of David on Israel's throne forever, forever, forever! This was the covenant God made through the prophet Nathan with David, according to 2 Samuel 7.

You and I may think it strange that any nation could believe such a thing. It seems naïve, gullible. We know that nothing on earth, no institution, is indestructible, and that no leadership succession is eternal. And yet, do we not wish mightily that we could make exactly that same covenant they believed they had made with God? Do we not pray that God will keep our nation secure, our city safe, our family well, and do not we presume that our presidential succession will endure long into the future? Will we not be wounded to the heart if any of these things fail? This covenant, I suggest, is high on our yearn-for list. Let us not think the ancients naïve; were they not but slightly different versions of us?

The Davidic covenant theology—belief in a secure Jerusalem and an eternal Davidic line—enjoyed enormous popularity in Israel for four hundred years. It was the foundation of the nation's faith. Songs sang it. Poetry recited it. Prophets proclaimed it. Priests preached it. Stories affirmed it. Events seemed to ratify it. When, in 715 BCE, the enormous army of Assyria's King Sennacherib surrounded Jerusalem ready to invade and destroy, the prophet Isaiah declared to a terrorized King Hezekiah, "Stand firm! God's promises to David are sure!" And, indeed, thousands in the Assyrian army died of some unknown affliction (the Bible says they were slain by an angel of the Lord). Sennacherib, without attacking, withdrew to Nineveh, where he was killed by his two sons. Any Israelite who doubted the Davidic covenant before this miraculous intervention certainly did not doubt it afterward!

When Nebuchadnezzar's enormous Babylonian army, in 587 BCE, surrounded Jerusalem preparing to invade, numerous voices once again proclaimed the certainty of the Davidic promises: "This is the temple of the Lord, the temple of the Lord, the temple of the Lord," and those voices inveighed, "No evil shall encroach here! No warfare shall breach our city walls." But this time the evil did encroach. After a blockade of the city, Nebuchadnezzar's force broke through the walls, overthrew its defenses, killed its soldiers, demolished its buildings, looted and destroyed its temple, ransacked its homes, and led most of its population into exile. In refugee camps near the Euphrates River they would spend the next forty-seven years. This was horrid trauma that would mark Israel's national consciousness for centuries to come. Had God forsaken Israel, rejected David? This was the question on every tongue. What had happened to God's promised steadfast love?

These critical questions are voiced in Psalm 89. Psalm 90 is the Psalms editors' response.

Psalm 89

This psalm, too long and repetitive to quote fully, divides into two distinct parts. Verses 1-37 form a joyous celebration of God's eternal covenant with David, celebrating the forever dependability of God's love. Verses 38-51 constitute a bitter lament over that covenant's failure.

The psalm opens with two verses proclaiming to the universe the eternal faithfulness of God.

> I will sing of your steadfast love, O LORD, forever;
>> with my mouth I will proclaim your faithfulness to all
>> generations.
> I declare that your steadfast love is established forever;
>> your faithfulness is as firm as the heavens. (vv. 1-2)

No matter what has happened, the overwhelming certainty for this psalmist is the everlasting assurance of God's steadfast love.

Verses 3 and 4 proclaim God's covenant with King David.

> I have made a covenant with my chosen one,
>> I have sworn to my servant David:
> "I will establish your descendants forever,
>> and build your throne for all generations."

Verses 5-18 extol the mighty works and the faithfulness of God, acclaimed by the creation, ruler of the ends of the earth. Happy are those who exult in the Lord's name!

Verses 19-37 move forward to detail God's promises to David. "The enemy shall not outwit him" (v. 22). "Forever I will keep my steadfast love for him" (v. 28). "I will establish his line forever" (v. 29). ". . . And his throne endure before me like the sun" (v. 36).

But, just when everything in the psalm seems wonderful and perfect, verse 38 turns a sharp, abrupt corner and sets before us the horrors of the present reality. "You have spurned and rejected him" (v. 38). "You have renounced the covenant" (v. 39). "You have exalted the right hand of his foes" (v. 42). "You have covered him with shame" (v. 45).

How long will our destitution last? verses 46-48 ask. We have only a short time on this earth; is this all we will ever again know?

And verses 49-51 mourn, Where has your steadfast love gone? We find it nowhere!

Psalm 89 is as deep a lament as the Bible offers! Lament over the death of the nation's core beliefs, of the most cherished confidences residing in the human heart. Psalm 89 squeezes and drains away all of the spirit's vitality.

It is absolutely remarkable that the psalm ends with verse 52: "Blessed be the LORD forever. Amen and Amen." From where in Israel's profoundly tortured faith this came is impossible to say. Except that it provides the introduction to the remainder of the Psalter. After Psalm 90, lament will nearly vanish and the Psalms will turn to praise, adoration, and exultation in the power and might of God. More on this will emerge in our subsequent study.

Psalm 90

90 LORD, you have been our dwelling place
    in all generations.
2 Before the mountains were brought forth,
    or ever you had formed the earth and the world,
    from everlasting to everlasting you are God.

3 You turn us back to dust,
    and say, "Turn back, you mortals."
4 For a thousand years in your sight
    are like yesterday when it is past,
    or like a watch in the night.

5 You sweep them away; they are like a dream,
    like grass that is renewed in the morning;
6 in the morning it flourishes and is renewed;
    in the evening it fades and withers.

7 For we are consumed by your anger;
    by your wrath we are overwhelmed.
8 You have set our iniquities before you,
    our secret lives in the light of your countenance.

9 For all our days pass away under your wrath;
    our years come to an end like a sigh.
10 The days of our life are seventy years,
    or perhaps eighty, if we are strong;
even though their span is only toil and trouble;
    they are soon gone, and we fly away.

11 Who considers the power of your anger?
    Your wrath is as great as the fear that is due you.
12 So teach us to count our days
    that we may gain a wise heart.

¹³   Turn, O Lord! How long?
        Have compassion on your servants!
¹⁴   Satisfy us in the morning with your steadfast love,
        so that we may rejoice and be glad all our days.
¹⁵   Make us glad as many days as you have afflicted us,
        and as many years as we have seen evil.
¹⁶   Let your work be manifest to your servants,
        and your glorious power to their children.
¹⁷   Let the favor of the Lord our God be upon us,
        and prosper for us the work of our hands—
        O prosper the work of our hands!

What does a nation do with crushing disillusionment, when its most precious beliefs seem to have been destroyed? What does a people do after the walls have been breached, the city sacked, the temple looted, and the most able of the population herded into exile? Where does Israel turn when horror has been heaped upon horror leading to mass deportation to a strange and distant place? What does a covenant community do when all the evidences indicate that God has abandoned them?

Psalm 90 is a search for some glimmer of hope amid the ruins of overwhelming destruction. It is a creation psalm prayer uttered from the nadir of Israel's wretched night.

Verses 1-2 begin with an invitation to rapt awe before God's eternity, to engagement with Genesis 1. But verses 3-4 quickly move to the futility of human life. We mortals occupy but a brief moment, returning quickly to the dust from which we were taken. But God is the God of eons, "from everlasting to everlasting." Our brevity and God's eternity—the contrast between the two—is the dominant subject of this psalm.

Verses 5-6 compare our lives with grass. Grass sparkles early in the day, fades late; we do too. (This grass metaphor for the human plight is employed several times in Scripture—see, for instance, Psalm 103:15-16 and Isaiah 40:6-7. It apparently painted a vivid image in the ancient consciousness.)

Verses 7-11 ponder the wrath of God turned against humans, how horrid and difficult it is. God's anger can burn like fire, consuming and overwhelming us. It turns the essence of life into toil and trouble, hard labor and difficulty, and then we die! This seems to be a clear picture of Israel's state of mind in exile.

Verse 12 is the focal point: "So teach us to count our days that we may gain a wise heart." From your eternity, illumine our brevity. From your "everlasting to everlasting," give wisdom to our threescore and ten years. May the immortal Teacher shine a lamp unto our mortal feet. Awe before the *glory* is the classroom for such learning. The massive Psalm 119 will later become an explication of this single verse from Psalm 90, and also a commentary on Psalm 1.

Verses 13-16 ask God to turn anger back into compassion, to mark every waking day with steadfast love, and to restore rejoicing and gladness among the people.

Verse 17 prays that God will make the labors of the people productive once again, bringing from human effort blessing instead of curse—a deep longing expressed many times in Scripture.

Following the laments and pleas for help scattered through Book III of the Psalms (Psalms 74, 79, 80, 83, 85, 86, 88, and 89), Psalm 90 replies: enter God's sanctuary! Soak yourself in radical amazement. The *glory* remains. God has not abandoned. Let's see if we can muster the strength to rise out of despair and move forward. Let the wisdom of the Holy One implant in us new direction and new devotion. Psalm 90 acknowledges the full depths of Israel's plight but then pleads with God to speak the creative word—"teach us!" (v. 12)—that will breathe new life into downtrodden lives.

Some years ago, the movie *Shawshank Redemption* portrayed a work-scene in a prison yard. Several dozen male inmates were scattered around the yard engaged in hard, grueling labor: digging, lifting, chopping, toting, etc. Suddenly, over a public address system designed for barking orders and commands across the yard, came the incomparably beautiful "Porgi, amor" from Mozart's *Marriage of Figaro*, a rich, contemplative soprano voice with orchestra beneath. Every inmate in the yard—brawny, tough, and cynical all around—stopped, transfixed, listening intensely, carried momentarily into a different dimension. The magic seized the entire yard. "What's going on here?" a prison official barked. "What the hell are they doing?" The work foreman, an inmate himself, replied something to the effect of, "The lady is looking at a beautiful place and singing about what she sees. The men can't see that place right now, but they sure appreciate her telling them about it." That is the role of Psalm 90 in response to Psalm 89, the role of the creation psalms in response to lament.

Psalm 89:52, as noted earlier, concludes the whole, "Blessed be the LORD forever. Amen and Amen." The remainder of the Psalter will amplify this note, concluding with a crescendo of six psalms (145–150) of total, undiluted praise.

Discussion Topics and Questions

1. Name some earthly securities that we presume, gifts from God that we cannot *imagine* would ever be taken away. Realize how many there are and how not-unusual was the covenant the ancients believed they had made with God. How often have you sought, deep in heart and soul, to make the same covenant?

2. Verses 36-51 of Psalm 89 express "abandonment," the experience of God's going away and leaving us totally alone. A slave laborer in a southern cotton field once sang to a sad, plaintive melody,

Sometimes I feel like a motherless child
sometimes I feel like a motherless child
sometimes I feel like a motherless child
A long ways from home
A long ways from home

Have you known this feeling? Can you write a verse or a sentence to express it? How did you find what was necessary to survive? How would you try to relate to someone else going through it?

3. An additional dynamic runs through the relation of Psalms 89 and 90. Psalm 90 is labeled, "A Prayer of Moses, the man of God." This is the only psalm in the Psalter that is ascribed to Moses (many were ascribed to David). The ascription suggests that Psalm 90 turns a distinct page in Israel's history (just as it opens Book IV in the Psalms). Formerly, the Davidic covenant of unconditional promises defined their relation to God, and David was their "forever" king. With Psalm 89, the Davidic covenant is gone. Israel has to look elsewhere for a covenant and a king. The ascription to Psalm 90 suggests that Israel was returning to the covenant made with Moses, long before David, the Deuteronomic covenant stated in Psalm 1. And the Psalm 90 text designates who the new king will be, "our

dwelling place in all generations"—God! Psalms 93–100, known as the "royal psalms," declare with resounding proclamation that God alone is Israel's king, that God is to be worshiped, praised, and lauded with full celebration. This theme carries forward through the rest of the book.

4. ". . . like grass that is renewed in the morning, . . . (but) in the evening . . . fades and withers" (vv. 5-6). Can you devise a similarly good metaphor to describe your own sense of our life's brevity?

5. Psalm 90:11 voices a frustrating, oft-asked question among the ancients: Why does our hard, earnest labor yield wheat but also weeds? Why is it possible for honest, sincere human efforts to produce outcomes exactly opposite of what was wanted? The Genesis narrative (Gen 3:17-18) includes this as a curse from God resulting from human sinfulness. Can you recall a story from your life when this has happened?

chapter five

PSALMS 137, 136, AND 138

My Own Intense Anger

This three-psalm cluster carries within it a deeply serious conversation. It tells us something about ourselves that we absolutely do not want to acknowledge (despite how accurate it is), but it also issues a delicate and sensitive word to people in our plight.

Psalm 137

137 By the rivers of Babylon—
   there we sat down and there we wept
   when we remembered Zion.
2   On the willows there
   we hung up our harps.
3   For there our captors
   asked us for songs,
   and our tormentors asked for mirth, saying,
   "Sing us one of the songs of Zion!"

4   How could we sing the LORD's song
   in a foreign land?
5   If I forget you, O Jerusalem,
   let my right hand wither!
6   Let my tongue cling to the roof of my mouth,
   if I do not remember you,
   if I do not set Jerusalem
   above my highest joy.

7   Remember, O LORD, against the Edomites
        the day of Jerusalem's fall,
     how they said, "Tear it down! Tear it down!
        Down to its foundations!"
8   O daughter Babylon, you devastator!
        Happy shall they be who pay you back
        what you have done to us!
9   Happy shall they be who take your little ones
        and dash them against the rock!

We begin in the middle of the cluster. Psalm 137 is nasty, horrible. I once reviewed a book manuscript in which the author wanted to delete it from the Bible because of how contrary its god seems to the biblical God. The psalm speaks of vengeance waged upon the innocent and helpless, of blind hatred. If the psalm is taken as a recommended behavior model, we end up despising enemies and murdering tiny babies. I once was asked to write a meditation on Psalm 137 for a booklet of Lenten devotionals. The editor refused my copy, declaring that it was too downbeat. That means I got the spirit of the psalm exactly right.

The setting is an exile camp on the Euphrates River in Babylon, many, many miles from "home" in Jerusalem. A sizable number of Israelites had been forcibly driven there after the destruction of 587 BCE. Settling in for a long stay, the exiles were brooding over recent events and the lives they now must live in this God-forsaken place. In verses 1-3, they recount their experience of arriving: cruel taunting! Back in their own land, Israel's confidence in God's covenant with David had been laced through their music. "Songs of Zion" they were called, tunes of mirth and celebration over the eternal security God promised to the Holy City. Psalms 46, 121, 122, 124, 125, and 132 are clear examples, and doubtless there were many more. These tunes would have been ubiquitous, flowing through the streets as hymns of the city's confidence. The youngest child to the oldest grandparent would have joined in: the Lord has chosen Zion, secure from the destructive violence of the surrounding world!

And now, with Jerusalem destroyed and Israel in exile, their captors taunted them with jeers, "Sing us one of your songs of Zion now!" Take up your harps, your stringed instruments, and perform one of those tunes you used to chant! Intone for us about how your deity surrounds your city with steadfast love and guarantees protection through all time!

All we could do, the psalmist says (vv. 4-6), was hang our harps on the willows and grieve, refusing to play or sing anything! Weeping instead of mirth! Mourning instead of celebration!

But let not our silence be mistaken as faithlessness. God's holy city is still our greatest delight, its memory living forever in our hearts.

And then verses 7-9 turn to consider a second grief piled upon the first. Edom was a close neighbor to Israel, a small kingdom to the southeast beyond the Dead Sea. Rich in iron and copper, Edom had for long periods been subjected to an Israelite domination that had drained the country's wealth. The most prosperous times in Israel's life had been fueled at Edomite expense. Thus did the Edomites feel requited when Babylon surrounded Jerusalem and destroyed it. Literally in view of the destruction, they had held a joyous party on a nearby hillside. Edom's taunts in that hour of chaotic overthrow were beyond horrible. The psalmist's wrathful reply was: blessed shall be those who seize your tiny, helpless babies and split open their skulls against the stones!

It is easy to see why Psalm 137 has been an outcast. It is hardly fuel for faithful spirits. But, as raw and horrible as the psalm is, let us remember that the Psalms editors chose to include it from many, many options. Its presence apparently bears a message the editors wanted us to hear.

Just preceding Psalm 137, the Psalms editors placed Psalm 136.

Psalm 136

136 O give thanks to the LORD, for he is good,
    for his steadfast love endures forever.
²   O give thanks to the God of gods,
    for his steadfast love endures forever.
³   O give thanks to the LORD of lords,
    for his steadfast love endures forever;

⁴   who alone does great wonders,
    for his steadfast love endures forever;
⁵   who by understanding made the heavens,
    for his steadfast love endures forever;

6   who spread out the earth on the waters,
         for his steadfast love endures forever;
7   who made the great lights,
         for his steadfast love endures forever;
8   the sun to rule over the day,
         for his steadfast love endures forever;
9   the moon and stars to rule over the night,
         for his steadfast love endures forever;

10   who struck Egypt through their firstborn,
         for his steadfast love endures forever;
11   and brought Israel out from among them,
         for his steadfast love endures forever;
12   with a strong hand and an outstretched arm,
         for his steadfast love endures forever;
13   who divided the Red Sea in two,
         for his steadfast love endures forever;
14   and made Israel pass through the midst of it,
         for his steadfast love endures forever;
15   but overthrew Pharaoh and his army in the Red Sea,
         for his steadfast love endures forever;
16   who led his people through the wilderness,
         for his steadfast love endures forever;
17   who struck down great kings,
         for his steadfast love endures forever;
18   and killed famous kings,
         for his steadfast love endures forever;
19   Sihon, king of the Amorites,
         for his steadfast love endures forever;
20   and Og, king of Bashan,
         for his steadfast love endures forever;
21   and gave their land as a heritage,
         for his steadfast love endures forever;
22   a heritage to his servant Israel,
         for his steadfast love endures forever.

23   It is he who remembered us in our low estate,
         for his steadfast love endures forever;
24   and rescued us from our foes,
         for his steadfast love endures forever;
25   who gives food to all flesh,
         for his steadfast love endures forever.

²⁶   O give thanks to the God of heaven,
        for his steadfast love endures forever.

Psalm 136, which may seem at first simply an arranged-for-liturgy review of the nation's history, is in fact a word spoken directly to Psalm 137. Three times at the beginning and once at the end, Psalm 136 bids us to "give thanks to the Lord." The psalm wants us to have hearts immersed in appreciation for God's gifts from creation until now. The prime gift? God's "steadfast love (which) endures forever." This refrain is stated twenty-six times through the psalm, in the second line of every verse. The psalm's intention is to bore this message solidly into our brains. This is exclamation beyond all extremes!

From verses 4 through 25, the psalm recites the history of God's creation of the universe (vv. 4-9), of Israel's deliverance from Egypt (vv. 10-15), of Israel's wilderness wandering and God's gift of the land (vv. 16-22), and of God's continuing care (vv. 23-25). The psalm's declaration is that the entire journey—from the creation until now—has been traveled on a road paved with God's steadfast love. Throughout, God's compassion has formed the way beneath our feet. The psalm calls all who are products of that journey to thanksgiving, to hearts of profound gratitude. Hardly could a twenty-six-verse poem be more single-focused.

And the editors follow Psalm 137 with Psalm 138.

Psalm 138

138   I give you thanks, O Lord, with my whole heart;
        before the gods I sing your praise;
²   I bow down toward your holy temple
        and give thanks to your name for your steadfast love and
            faithfulness;
        for you have exalted your name and your word
        above everything.
³   On the day I called, you answered me,
        you increased my strength of soul.

⁴   All the kings of the earth shall praise you, O Lord,
        for they have heard the words of your mouth.
⁵   They shall sing of the ways of the Lord,
        for great is the glory of the Lord.

6   For though the LORD is high, he regards the lowly;
        but the haughty he perceives from far away.

7   Though I walk in the midst of trouble,
        you preserve me against the wrath of my enemies;
    you stretch out your hand,
        and your right hand delivers me.
8   The LORD will fulfill his purpose for me;
        your steadfast love, O LORD, endures forever.
    Do not forsake the work of your hands.

Psalm 138 also is an invitation to give thanks for God's steadfast love, a companion to Psalm 136. Here, however, God's steadfast love is mentioned twice instead of twenty-six times. The focus is elsewhere: on God's empathy and care for the weak. "Though the LORD is high, he regards the lowly" (v. 6) is the centerpiece. The kings of earth in all their resplendent power bow in praise for the high Lord, but it is a great surprise when they realize that God regards the lowly over the mighty, slaves over kings. The psalm personalizes this divine attribute, affirming that when I am lowly, walking in the midst of trouble, God preserves me against the wrath of my enemies, stretching out God's right hand to deliver me. As with Psalm 136, this psalm is a call to have a heart of profound gratitude.

The Three-Psalm Cluster

One morning in a town where we lived, a family prepared their three children to go to school and sent them out to the nearby corner school bus stop. With light rain falling, the children sought cover under the bus stop shelter. As they waited, a young man, legally drunk, who had just had a morning fight with his girlfriend, came driving down the street at an undetermined speed. He cut the corner sharply, jumped the curb, took down two metal sign posts, crossed the sidewalk, and mowed over the school bus shelter, killing all three children. I did not know the family, but I am certain that out of the entire book of Psalms, Psalm 137 would have best spoken for those parents that morning.

As loathsome and wretched as Psalm 137 is, the deeply disturbing fact is that all of us, every single one, is capable of uttering it—in a similar circumstance. It conveys emotions that remain mostly hidden but firmly planted in us. The Psalms editors knew this. The editors had heard the rage coming from people in that time, including the self. *This psalm is us,* the editors are saying by placing it in the book. We are asked to acknowledge that unattractive fact. Our faith, the editors are saying, needs to include our relationship to our own intense anger. Stop for a moment and be sure you absorb that. *Our faith needs to include our relationship to our own intense anger!* This is the message of Psalm 137.

The remarkable characteristic of the Psalms 136–138 cluster, however, is in what happens next: exceptional! The editors could well have accompanied Psalm 137 with warnings and admonitions against anger. Psalm 37:8-9:

> Refrain from anger, and forsake wrath.
>   Do not fret—it leads only to evil.
> For the wicked shall be cut off,
>   but those who wait for the Lord shall inherit the land.

(The editors could easily have placed the whole of Psalm 37 as a moralistic reply to Psalm 137.) Proverbs 16:32 was another possibility: "One who is slow to anger is better than the mighty, and one whose temper is controlled than one who captures a city." Or Proverbs 19:11: "Those with good sense are slow to anger, and it is their glory to overlook an offense." Or the ancient saying: "Whom the gods would destroy, they first make mad." But the Psalms editors seem to know that moral maxims are trite and patronizing against the atrocities that produced Psalm 137. While your city is being sacked and burned, and you yourself are being driven forcibly into a foreign refugee camp, the admonition, "Don't get angry!" is appallingly banal. Rather than attaching a moral maxim, the editors placed Psalms 136 and 138 on either side of Psalm 137. And what that placement conveys is nothing short of magnificent.

The editors are saying: despite the hell of our recent past, we have always been, and will always be surrounded on every side by God's deep compassion! As hard and miserable and difficult and wretched as life has been, divine grace remains our dominant companion. The midst of our savage fury is not the time for working out what that needs to mean for us. Tomorrow may be better for moral reasoning than today. But our theology still speaks. Let us believe in our hearts that even through hell God's compassion surrounds us. Nothing can take that away.

The only behavior urged by Psalms 136 and 138 is, "Give thanks. . . ." Faith is a gratitude grounded deeply in the human soul.

Now comes your second sermon assignment. This time I give you nine words, because the assignment is more challenging. The single point of your sermon is to be: what the Psalms editors are saying to us by placing Psalm 137 between Psalms 136 and 138. What is the message in enveloping our blistering vitriol within God's unending compassion? Your added challenge is that I expect you to be as discerning as the Psalms editors were. No moralizing! No telling your hypothetical congregation what they *should* or *shouldn't* do. Preach what the Psalms editors preached. Place Psalm 137 between Psalms 136 and 138, strongly and vividly, and then let your congregation, in their own time, figure out for themselves what they are to do, realizing that right now may not be the best time for forming that judgment. Write your nine-word (or fewer) sermon sentence before you read further.

Here is my sermon: *Surrounding my fiercest anger is God's greatest love.* I can see exactly how that sermon will lay out. It will fully allow the anger, but it will suggest that there is a transcending story. That story may need time to emerge.

I stand amazed at the ancient Psalms editors' savvy and insight.

Discussion Topics and Questions

1. Recall a time when Psalm 137 has spoken for you. What has moved you through and beyond that moment?

2. Recall a time when you have correctly said to yourself, "I need to wait before I react." A time when you did, a time when you didn't. What happened? What did you learn?

3. Recall a time when you have been overwhelmingly aware of God's continuing care and love for you, that your entire life has been traveled on a highway paved with God's steadfast love. Do you ever let that thought envelop your whole mind, filling your senses with gratitude?

4. The clustering of Psalms 136, 137, and 138 illustrates a key and vital point in biblical interpretation. Believers have often looked at the Bible as primarily a book of behavior norms, asking quickly of every text, "What are we supposed to do?" The Ten Commandments, the Sermon on the Mount, the covenant code of Exodus, the Mosaic books of Deuteronomy and Leviticus, the teachings of Jesus, the admonitions of Paul: these tend to make the Bible look like a massive collection of God's directives for our behavior. I, myself, used to think of the Bible that way.

But no longer. I now ask different questions of biblical texts and get what I find to be much richer results. When reading a text, my first two questions are: What does this text tell us about us, ourselves, and what does it tell us about God? What is the anthropology portrayed? What is the theology? A text may speak of one, the other, or both.

After—*only* after!—I have answered these two questions do I proceed to the third: What ethic does this text call for? What does it want us to do? My ancient, deeply embedded tendency is to jump immediately to this question #3, and it is critical that I stop myself. For the fact is that with full portraits of the anthropology and the theology of a text, question #3 may be unnecessary. The Bible's dominant ethic is, "Do what God has done," and often that will have become entirely evident without explanation. Explanation, in fact, becomes trite and trivial, fodder for a moralistic sermon.

The cluster of Psalms 136–138 illustrates this vividly. Psalm 137 is full of anthropology. We see our raw selves, how vindictively angry we can get when severely wronged. There is almost no theology in the psalm except the implied message that God hears and tolerates even our most savage prayers. If we jump immediately to extract an ethic from the psalm, we get a horror: surely God does not will us to hate taunters and crack the skulls of enemy babies.

Psalms 136 and 138 tell us richly about God. From the beginning of creation until now, God has paved a highway of steadfast love for our journey. God's abundant love possesses special empathy for the lowly, the downtrodden, and the oppressed, continuing to visit us in our deepest despair.

Placing my capacity for hostility and anger beside God's ages-long steadfast love—that is, contrasting who I am with who God is—leaves little doubt as to what I am called to do. For me to spell it out would be needless moralism; the congregation is intelligent and will know. And what they know will be far more profound than any collection of dos and don'ts I might assemble. A well-told, biblically based God-and-us story most often needs no ethical explication.

chapter six

PSALMS 72 AND 82

God's Great Passion

Psalms 72 and 82 address the same issue from two entirely different perspectives, forming together a rich portrait of what the Bible considers to be God's great passion.

Psalm 72

72 Give the king your justice, O God,
    and your righteousness to the king's son.
2 May he judge your people with righteousness,
    and your poor with justice.
3 May the mountains yield prosperity for the people,
    and the hills, in righteousness.
4 May he defend the cause of the poor of the people,
    give deliverance to the needy,
    and crush the oppressor.

5 May he live while the sun endures,
    and as long as the moon, throughout all generations.
6 May he be like rain that falls on the mown grass,
    like showers that water the earth.
7 In his days may righteousness flourish
    and peace abound, until the moon is no more.

8 May he have dominion from sea to sea,
    and from the River to the ends of the earth.
9 May his foes bow down before him,
    and his enemies lick the dust.

10   May the kings of Tarshish and of the isles
      render him tribute,
   may the kings of Sheba and Seba
      bring gifts.
11   May all kings fall down before him,
      all nations give him service.

12   For he delivers the needy when they call,
      the poor and those who have no helper.
13   He has pity on the weak and the needy,
      and saves the lives of the needy.
14   From oppression and violence he redeems their life;
      and precious is their blood in his sight.

15   Long may he live!
      May gold of Sheba be given to him.
   May prayer be made for him continually,
      and blessings invoked for him all day long.
16   May there be abundance of grain in the land;
      may it wave on the tops of the mountains;
      may its fruit be like Lebanon;
   and may people blossom in the cities
      like the grass of the field.
17   May his name endure forever,
      his fame continue as long as the sun.
   May all nations be blessed in him;
      may they pronounce him happy.

18   Blessed be the LORD, the God of Israel,
      who alone does wondrous things.
19   Blessed be his glorious name forever;
      may his glory fill the whole earth.
   Amen and Amen.

Psalm 72 is a prayer for the king addressed to God. It asks for many of the things any subjects might request for their monarch: long life (vv. 5, 15a), dominion far and wide (vv. 8-11), riches (v. 15b), the prayers of the people (v. 15c), prosperity (vv. 3, 6, 16), and fame (v. 17). But these blessings, the psalm makes clear, are conditional upon the king's living up to several standards set by God: he is to "deliver the needy when they call, the poor and those who have no helper" (v. 12). He is to "have pity on the weak and the needy, and (save) the lives of the needy" (v. 13). He is to redeem their lives "from oppression and violence," and "their blood" is to be "precious . . . in his sight" (v. 14). The psalm prays that Israel's monarch shall embody a deep sense of justice and righteousness (v. 1), empathy for the poor (v. 2), advocacy for the poor and needy, crushing the oppressor (v. 4). Thus will he be "like rain that falls on the mown grass, like showers that water the earth" (v. 6). Thus will "righteousness flourish and peace abound, until the moon is no more" (v. 7).

Psalm 72 reflects the astounding, world-inverting character of Israel's theology: that the king will prosper and the land will flourish *as long as* the king's reign strongly embodies God's empathy for the poor, the widow, the orphan, and the slave. Lobbyists representing various power interests will cluster around the king seeking special consideration, asking for this, for that, seeking to trade political favor for economic favor (we know the scene!) Amid this influence-clamor, the king's heart is to make him without fail the chief lobbyist for the poorest of the land, protecting their interests and answering their needs. As long as the king represents God's empathy, Psalm 72 is saying, Israel shall flourish with vigor and goodness and peace. The clear implication is that if the king does not do that, Israel will disintegrate and die beneath the corruption of his rule, plundered and despoiled by nations round about.

A clearer picture of God could not be drawn: devoted empathy for the powerless is God's heart and soul, and God wants the monarch to rule in exactly the same way. I wonder sometimes why presidents, governors, and mayors who, in running for office, depict themselves as faithful believers, once elected, ignore or forget that campaigning on the merits of Psalm 72 is what got them there.

Psalm 82

> 82 God has taken his place in the divine council;
> in the midst of the gods he holds judgment:
> 2 "How long will you judge unjustly
> and show partiality to the wicked?
> 3 Give justice to the weak and the orphan;
> maintain the right of the lowly and the destitute.
> 4 Rescue the weak and the needy;
> deliver them from the hand of the wicked."

5   They have neither knowledge nor understanding,
        they walk around in darkness;
        all the foundations of the earth are shaken.

6   I say, "You are gods,
        children of the Most High, all of you;
7   nevertheless, you shall die like mortals,
        and fall like any prince."

8   Rise up, O God, judge the earth;
        for all the nations belong to you!

If Psalm 72 showed us an earth scene, Psalm 82 reveals the corresponding heaven scene. The setting is a meeting of what the psalm calls "the divine council," God's collection of lesser gods whose function is to implement on earth God's policies. (No, this is not a challenge to monotheism. The Bible refers repeatedly to lesser gods who are to carry out God's wishes. As this psalm will show clearly, however, they are not competitor-gods but sub-gods. Only one God rules in the creation!)

God takes a seat at the head of the council table with the lesser gods gathered around. One question dominates the meeting: "How long will you judge unjustly and show partiality to the wicked?" (v. 2). These lesser gods, "children of the Most High" (v. 6), it seems, have been siding with the wicked in their court cases against the innocent, exonerating merchants who cheat, defrauding widows, exploiting orphans, going along with what humans are doing rather than challenging.

> Give justice to the weak and the orphan;
>   maintain the right of the lowly and the destitute.
> Rescue the weak and the needy;
>   deliver them from the hand of the wicked. (vv. 3-4)

God then passes verdict on these recalcitrant inferiors;

> I say, "You are gods,
>   children of the Most High, all of you;
> nevertheless, you shall die like mortals,
>   and fall like any prince." (vv. 6-7)

Ejected from the divine council! Cast down to become like humans! No longer worthy as God's servants! Not only will earth see a drastic rearrangement because of ill treatment of the weak but heaven also. God has no tolerance for divine power that ignores the lowly.

The final verse of Psalm 82 is a prayer for God to act quickly.

The portrait drawn here of God's strong compassion for the lowly reflects many, many other texts across the Bible. The law codes in Exodus (21:1-11; 22:25-27; 23:6-8; 23:10-13; plus others), Leviticus (25:8-12; 25:39-46; plus others), and Deuteronomy (14:28-29; 15:7-11, 12-18; 16:9-15; 25:13-16; plus others) express a deep and oft-repeated concern for human beings most in need. Amos (5:10-13, 21-24; 6:4-6; 8:4-6), Micah (2:1-3; 6:1-16), and Isaiah (3:13-15; 5:8-10; 10:1-4) all see God as intensely empathetic with society's weakest, and they castigate Israel when the nation does not share that concern. Many psalms (10:1-18; 68; 109; 112:5-10; 138; and more) reflect the same theology. God—the Bible professes repeatedly and widely—bears deep in God's soul serious concern for the lowly and dispossessed, wanting for them justice, mercy, and sharing.

Where did this picture of God come from? How did God's people come to perceive it? It did not come from the religions of surrounding nations. Israel did a lot of borrowing from other religions, but not this. The Bible tells us clearly where it came from. Exodus 23:9: "You shall not oppress a resident alien; you know the heart of the alien, for you were aliens in the land of Egypt." Deuteronomy 10:19: "You shall . . . love the stranger, for you were strangers in the land of Egypt," (plus many other texts). Israel discerned God's heart through what God did for Israel in Egypt: delivering poor slaves to freedom and prosperity.

The gods, in Egypt's eyes, had visited their nation many times before. They came to share with Egypt's rulers divine advice on how to rule. As the gods' earthly representatives, the Pharaohs were to pattern their government and dominion on divine government and dominion. Egypt was to be run the way heaven was. A special channel of communication for precisely this purpose was carefully maintained.

But when the God of Israel visited Egypt, it was on an entirely different mission. *God came not to consult with Pharaoh on how to rule but to consult with Pharaoh's slaves on how to escape.* God came to relate not with the kings but with the outcasts, to spend time not in the royal palace but roaming the huts and hovels of Egypt's slave ghettos. Unheard of! Revolutionary! A totally new concept of divinity! Egypt's gods would never lower themselves to such depths, only one God. This visit created something entirely new on the human stage. The ancient near eastern world had never seen the likes: a God who cares most about the people the humans don't care about. The domain of religion took on a different cast. Royalty beware! The world has inverted!

God's intense empathy for the lowly and powerless would radiate into the New Testament (and indeed far beyond). Matthew 25:40: ". . . just as you did it to one of the least of these who are members of my family, you did it to me." Mark 10:45: "For the Son of Man came not to be served but to serve, and to give his life . . ." Luke 4:18-21: "The Spirit of the LORD is upon me, because he has anointed me to bring good news to the poor. . . , to let the oppressed go free, to proclaim the year of the LORD's favor. . . . Today this scripture has been fulfilled in your hearing." Many other New Testament texts also state the same message.

Someone has said that if you scissor from a Bible all the texts that express God's empathy for the downcast, you end up with Swiss cheese.

According to these many texts, the church and the synagogue have been issued a major challenge. Psalms 72 and 82 take their place at the center of that challenge.

Discussion Topics and Questions

1. Several years ago a man in a Sunday school class, after I had presented this picture, said, "I believe that if you take all the money in the world and divide it equally among all the human beings, it will only be a short time before we return to essentially the same wealth distribution we have today. As Jesus said, 'The poor you always have with you.'" How do you respond to the man's comment?

2. Andrew Carnegie, in his "gospel of wealth," set forth his belief that God appoints certain individuals, gives them superior intelligence and insight, and lays on them the responsibility of amassing as much wealth as they can, by whatever means, and then spending that wealth to lift the masses out of their naturally depressed state into higher and better lives. Carnegie did not believe that most people possess the intelligence to do this for themselves, that, given wealth, they will waste it frivolously feeding their petty desires. Thus did Carnegie see himself called to gather a huge fortune in the steel industry (much of it on the backs of low-paid, vastly ill-treated laborers), gain full billing as one of the late-nineteenth-century American "robber barons," and then expend major portions of his wealth building public libraries in cities and towns across the country. Reading books, Carnegie believed, would lift the masses upward. He also stated that he would never leave a single dime to any of his children since history had shown clearly the wreckage that inherited wealth can create. How would you evaluate Carnegie's "gospel of wealth?" (I, by the way, understand Ayn Rand as essentially a non-religious version of Andrew Carnegie.)

3. Some Americans believe that Social Security is exceedingly helpful in keeping millions of retired people out of poverty, and that it takes a strong, positive step in reflecting the Bible's understanding of God's empathy for the lowly. Other Americans believe that Social Security and similar "social net" programs make people financially dependent on the government and less responsible in taking care of themselves. What do you think?

4. "The prosperity gospel," the belief that faith can implant in us a power to become economically successful, is increasingly popular across America today. How do you respond?

5. Many a church across this country has long understood that part of its Bible-based mission is to help struggling, dispossessed people, usually quietly and without advertisement. What efforts of this sort have you been a part of?

chapter seven

PSALMS 51, 106, AND 32

Finding a New Heart

Scattered throughout the book of Psalms, these three psalms construct a single picture critically pertinent to their time and ours. The Psalms editors could have clustered them side by side, increasing the focus, but the scattering suggests that what they deal with happens throughout life, not just in episodes. Several other psalms scattered through (the so-called "penitential psalms," 6, 38, 102, 130, and 143) inject the same message more briefly.

The theme is: owning up to the moral flaw within us, admitting our evil. There is a duality we need to keep in mind as we proceed through this study, a two-faceted understanding of ourselves. You and I see people everywhere embody a great capacity for good. In large quantity, benevolence resides in us. Everywhere I have traveled in the world—from rural Maine, to small-village Mississippi, to Inverness, to downtown Jerusalem, to the markets of Guatemala City, to isolated settlements in rural Nicaragua—I have found good-hearted people ready to be friendly and to extend help if needed. This to me is one of the great hopes for our planet: that everyday people the world over are far more generous and kind-hearted than the headline news coverage often suggests. Good resides richly in human lives!

Evil also resides there, a flaw. We can be self-centered, haughty, arrogant. We can ignore others in need. We can manipulate, deceive, and oppress, waging intense cruelty. Our darker side never stops.

Both these capacities live in us. But when focusing on the flawed side, as we shall do here, it is easy to get so immersed that we drown in it, disregarding the good. To conclude that we are little more than "filthy rags," as one faith statement used to say, is plainly not accurate! The healthiest lives I relate to—which are many—are people who are fully aware of the evil in us, but who are also quite capable and confident in their goodness. They do not live lives plagued by guilt and inadequacy but motivated forward by self-trust. To be a person drowned in self-recrimination helps nothing and no one. Full awareness of our dual nature needs to stay with us throughout this study.

Psalm 51

51   Have mercy on me, O God,
      according to your steadfast love;
  according to your abundant mercy
      blot out my transgressions.
2   Wash me thoroughly from my iniquity
      and cleanse me from my sin.

3   For I know my transgressions,
      and my sin is ever before me.
4   Against you, you alone, have I sinned,
      and done that which is evil in your sight,
  so that you are justified in your sentence
      and blameless when you pass judgment.
5   Indeed, I was born guilty,
      a sinner when my mother conceived me.

6   You desire truth in the inward being;
      therefore teach me wisdom in my secret heart.
7   Purge me with hyssop, and I shall be clean;
      wash me and I shall be whiter than snow.
8   Let me hear joy and gladness;
      let the bones that you have crushed rejoice.
9   Hide your face from my sins,
      and blot out all my iniquities.

10   Create in me a clean heart, O God,
      and put a new and right spirit within me.
11   Do not cast me away from your presence,
      and do not take your holy spirit from me.

12   Restore to me the joy of your salvation,
         and sustain in me a willing spirit.

13   Then I will teach transgressors your ways,
         and sinners will return to you.
14   Deliver me from bloodshed, O God,
         O God of my salvation,
         and my tongue will sing aloud of your deliverance.

15   O Lord, open my lips,
         and my mouth will declare your praise.
16   For you have no delight in sacrifice;
         if I were to give a burnt offering, you would not be pleased.
17   The sacrifice acceptable to God is a broken spirit;
         a broken and contrite heart, O God, you will not despise.

18   Do good to Zion in your good pleasure;
         rebuild the walls of Jerusalem,
19   then you will delight in right sacrifices,
         in burnt offerings and whole burnt offerings;
         then bulls will be offered on your altar.

Psalm 51 is a beautiful poetic portrait, the only trouble being that the subject is hard and anguishing: my sin. I do wrong, the psalm says. There is a relentless self-centeredness deep within me.

Verses 1-2 begin pointedly in the middle of the subject, no tiptoeing around, no easing in. Four earnest and heartfelt requests, all asking the same thing: God's mercy and cleansing. There's no question in this text that I need it, no qualifications. *In me resides serious guilt*, and the full agenda is my begging God's forgiveness and renewal.

The superscription labels the work, "A Psalm of David, when the prophet Nathan came to him, after he had gone in to Bathsheba." Recounted in 2 Samuel 11-12, the great King David, at the pinnacle of his power and success, had forced the wife of a loyal soldier in his army to have sex with him because of her alluring beauty. On learning that she was pregnant, David concocted an elaborate plot, finally having her husband killed in battle and claiming Bathsheba as his own. David's chief court prophet, Nathan, risked his life by confronting the king and declaring God's condemnation of what he had done. David sought to repent. Psalm 51 is presented as his psalm of repentance. Neither the author of the 2 Samuel 11-12 story nor the Psalms editors seem to have had any notion of letting David off lightly, even though (especially because!) he was king.

Verses 3-5 reiterate that no one else is to blame, just me. And, most of all, my sin is against you, God. Yes, also against people around me, reaping grievous and miserable results in human lives, but foremost against you. I have forsaken the trust you placed in me. "So that you are justified in your sentence and blameless when you pass judgment. Indeed, I was born guilty, a sinner when my mother conceived me." The flaw was built into me from my very beginning, and it is an inescapable part of my constitution.

Note that verse 5 has, in the past, been translated, "in sin did my mother conceive me" (RSV, for instance). That single line led entire generations before us to suspect that human sexual activity was sinful, that only chastity created a pure life. A small country church I once served, a Scottish Presbyterian community with names like McCormick, McDonald, McKell, Mateer, McArn, McAvery, and McBee, included one household of four unmarried brothers and sisters who had resided together all their adult lives because they took Psalm 51:5 literally. The family died out, of course. We can be thankful for the more accurate modern translation.

Verses 6-9 beg for cleansing, for wisdom, for purging, for washing.

Verses 10-12 seek restoration, renewal. The Hebrew word "create," with which the section begins, is the same word used in Genesis 1 for what God did originally in creating the universe. Start over, the psalmist is saying. Return to the beginning and launch me anew. That's what it will take to bring about the new person I need to become.

Verses 13-17 are a promise to preach and proclaim.

Verses 18-19 are a postexilic ending, obviously an add-on from a later date than the original psalm.

In Psalm 51 as a whole, we stand before God and acknowledge: I have sinned grievously, there is a profound moral flaw in my being that I cannot overcome. Forgive me! Cleanse me! Re-create a new person from me! Restore me to joy! I present to you a broken spirit and a contrite heart in hope that you will reclaim alienated me as your own.

The task posed by Psalm 51 is one of the hardest in human life: honest self-reflection. To cover blame for our flaws, we humans tend to construct an entire range of dodges, alibis, distractions, and deflections. We are masters of Adam's second sin: blaming it on Eve. This psalm asks us to look directly and honestly at ourselves and confess to God: the blame doesn't go to Tom, Dick, or Harriet; I am guilty! I did it! The psalm presses this point.

Psalm 51 also sets forth the confidence that God is a God of forgiveness with the power and the will to take the wretched parts of me and fashion a new self. There is no depravity too miserable for God to redeem. That is the striking good news in the psalm: my redemption is possible!

Psalm 106

Psalm 106 is Psalm 51 spoken by the nation rather than by an individual. A collective admission rather than a personal one. Nations, as we know, do evil, often as a by-product of something they believe is good. Psalm 106 details, step by step (vv. 6-43), what the psalm writer considers grievous misdeeds running through Israel's history. We may not concur in all that writer's judgments ("They did not destroy the peoples, as the LORD commanded them," v. 34, for instance), but we have to honor the overall intention: to acknowledge that our nation stands guilty of evil before God, and that we need to have clear view of our involvement. Nations also do not easily make such admissions. Historians have identified *the myth of innocence* as one of the founding images on which our own country was built (see, for instance, *The Burden of Southern History*, C. Vann Woodward), and we are by no means alone in making this claim. Nations around the world offer prayers to God asking for favor and blessing ("God Bless America" is one of ours), but never—never!—do these prayers include a confession of our own national wrongdoing. Psalm 106 is a rare moment of honesty. Any national leadership that does not, in its strategy and planning, engage in a sober evaluation of its own capacity for evil stands in danger of waging a cruel hubris on the world.

Psalm 32

32 Happy are those whose transgression is forgiven,
    whose sin is covered.
2 Happy are those to whom the LORD imputes no iniquity,
    and in whose spirit there is no deceit.

3   While I kept silence, my body wasted away
          through my groaning all the day long.
4   For day and night your hand was heavy upon me;
          my strength was dried up as by the heat of summer.

5   Then I acknowledged my sin to you,
          and I did not hide my iniquity;
      I said, "I will confess my transgressions to the LORD,"
          and you forgave the guilt of my sin.

6   Therefore let all who are faithful
          offer prayer to you;
      at a time of distress, the rush of mighty waters
          shall not reach them.
7   You are a hiding place for me;
          you preserve me from trouble;
          you surround me with glad cries of deliverance.

8   I will instruct you and teach you the way you should go;
          I will counsel you with my eye upon you.
9   Do not be like a horse or a mule, without understanding;
          whose temper must be curbed with bit and bridle,
          else it will not stay near you.

10   Many are the torments of the wicked,
          but steadfast love surrounds those who trust in the LORD.
11   Be glad in the LORD and rejoice, O righteous,
          and shout for joy, all you upright in heart.

Psalm 32 is a psalm of joy and happiness that the guilt slate has been wiped clean, sin forgiven. "While I kept silence" (v. 3), that is, while I bottled my misdeeds up inside myself and feigned innocence, "my body wasted away." "For day and night your hand was heavy upon me" (v. 4). My stubborn refusal exacted its price. I wanted to ignore my guilt, but your all-knowing presence weighed mightily upon me. My body dried up as a plant scorched by blazing sun.

"Then I acknowledged my sin to you . . . , and you forgave the guilt of my sin" (v. 5). Your forgiveness blew across my life as a refreshing wind. And now I am a new person, redeemed and re-created by you! Now I sing with a joyous heart. "Happy are those whose transgression is forgiven" (v. 1).

Don't be dumb as a horse, stubborn as a mule! Take heed! Make Psalm 51 a prayer you are able to pray to God.

The Psalm Group

The Bible does some astounding things, and here we encounter one of the most astounding! A key figure in the Bible's story is Israel's founder, the great, magnificent, incomparable King David whose life is depicted across the book of 2 Samuel. David was superb! He defeated the giant Goliath. He rescued failing Israel from the hands of the mentally inept King Saul. He created an army with which he systematically defeated the adversaries round about. He seized Mount Zion from the Jebusites to found Jerusalem, the Holy City, as his capital. So pleased was God with this brilliant, able young king that God carved an eternal covenant with him, guaranteeing to make Jerusalem the divine dwelling place forever, to protect it from all harm and danger as long as the sun endures. God promised that the Davidic line of kings would rule through all generations, enjoying the full protection of God's steadfast love. The story told of King David in 2 Samuel is nearly unending in its praise and adulation.

But then comes chapter 11, miserable, horrible chapter 11. We see here a David consumed by illicit passion, using the full power of his office to secure his self-centered craving, disregarding the life and person of the woman who is the object of his lust, scheming to kill one of the most honorable soldiers in his army, and then plotting to cover it up. Any Davidic virtue presented earlier is more than obliterated. The only thing he does well is not kill the prophet Nathan when Nathan confronts him. Psalm 51 is presented to us as David's prayer of confession after Nathan's confrontation.

The most amazing factor is that the writer/editor of 2 Samuel included this affair in the biblical account. That writer/editor could easily have left it out, as the creator of the parallel story of David's life in Chronicles did. *You simply didn't display for public consumption the dark side of your super-hero king*! This was not the way biographical story was written. You wanted to present a role model, a story lesser members of the kingdom would look up to and seek to emulate. Not the whole story. Surely, we all have our darker sides; we all know that. But faith needs to be upbeat! So we are often told.

And even more amazing is that this David story sets the tone for the rest of the Bible. Whenever the Bible tells of some highly prominent figure, without fail it records heroism and flaw, roses and thorns. Abraham was the great father of faith who, at God's call, left home, family, and country to settle in a land of God's bidding, not knowing the result. Abraham also, on entering Egypt, lied that his beautiful wife Sarah was his sister, fearful that the Egyptians would kill him and seize her if they discovered the truth. Hardly a role model!

Jacob, the patriarch for whom the nation Israel was named, was a schemer from before he was born, contesting with his twin brother Esau over who could get out first, cheating Esau of his birthright and their father's blessing, swindling his Uncle Laban, and wrestling with an angel of God in his quest for a divine blessing. Hardly a role model!

Moses, the great prophet who led Israel out of Egypt, was first a fugitive murderer, having killed an Egyptian and fled into Sinai to escape.

Solomon, the wise king who turned Israel into an economic giant, had his wisdom fail miserably when he conscripted slave labor from his own northern tribes and proceeded to split Israel in half from the intense rebellion.

The nation Israel, after it escaped Egyptian slavery at the Red Sea and danced in celebration on the eastern bank, turned quickly into a nation of complainers, bickering over water and food, and finally, at Mount Sinai, fashioning a golden calf to replace the God who had brought them out of Egypt.

Simon, given the name Peter, the solid rock on which the church was founded, first and foremost among the disciples, denied Jesus three times from fear that he himself would be arrested and prosecuted.

Paul, dedicated Christian missionary to the Mediterranean world, a committed disciple of the living Christ, wrote to the church in Rome,

> So I find it to be a law that when I want to do what is good, evil lies close at hand. For I delight in the law of God in my inmost self, but I see in my members another law at war with the law of my mind, making me captive to the law of sin that dwells in my members. Wretched man that I am! Who will

rescue me from this body of death? Thanks be to God through Jesus Christ our LORD! So then, with my mind I am a slave to the law of God, but with my flesh I am a slave to the law of sin. (Rom 7:21-25)

The four gospel writers depict the twelve disciples of Christ not as hero figures to be emulated by the later church but primarily as half-witted souls who "get it" only very slowly, weaving their own ego-driven agendas through the events of their discipleship. Not one of these is a role model!

In the Bible there seems to be an eleven-hundred-year conspiracy that no great king, no great leader, no highly significant human figure will have his/her biography told only in part. We display the whole life, not just a flattering part. The influence that kept that literary policy in place from 1000 BCE through 100 CE is absolutely amazing, whatever it was. The human psyche embodies a strong tendency to deny guilt, not to confess it, but a whole succession of biblical writers counters this trend.

And the clear message is that Psalms 51 and 106 need to become regular prayers for us. We are called to acknowledge the sin we commit, both as individuals and a nation. As well as lots of good things, we do bad things, and we are a danger to the world if we don't know it.

The biblical tradition has spawned numerous "theologies" through the years: Roman theology, Lutheran theology, Reformed theology, liberation theology, feminist theology, process theology, to name only a few. After years of interaction with that menu, I have come to believe that the most critical question to be posed to every theology is: Does it urge its adherents to confess their own flaws? Does it treat me, us, along with other people, as part of the problem? If not, then, first, the theology isn't biblical, and, second, it is set to wage destructive arrogance on the world.

The fundamental issue is whether we will take responsibility for ourselves and our actions. Am I to blame for the bad things I do or is someone else? Over nearly four decades as a pastor, I would periodically invite psychotherapists in the congregation—usually two or three a year—to lunch to ask a single question: "Tell me how the fundamental human pathology is showing up in your office these days. We people have a moral flaw within us; how is it currently manifesting itself in your practice?" One answer, through the years, always dominated: we work constantly at getting people to be accountable for their own actions. People want to blame their own bad stuff on other people, other influences. One small example I overheard in a doctor's office. Doctor to male patient: "You have got to lose weight!" Male patient, pointing to wife: "You'll have to talk to her about that." Doctor: "She doesn't need to lose weight; you do!" Psalm 51 is abundantly clear. I am the one responsible, not someone else. Me, number one. It is a word the Bible will not let us overlook.

Discussion Topics and Questions

1. Sometimes, having strong faith has been characterized as *knowing that I am right,* possessing strong convictions and holding to them firmly. Given the Bible-wide picture developed above, I contend that strong faith consists as much or more of *knowing that I can be wrong*, of living a life that practices honest self-criticism and avoids unbending certainty. What do you make of my contention?

2. For many people, guilt is associated with a deep feeling of shame and inadequacy implanted in them during childhood, something they have spent the rest of their lives trying to overcome. They have a very hard time thinking of a confession of sin as helpful and creative in their lives. Confession becomes a how-awful-I-am wallowing. How much is this built into you? Are you able to be genuinely self-critical without submerging yourself in self-criticism and self-doubt, or does it set off too many deeply implanted, ancient scripts in you?

3. There are a great many organizations in American society that, when they meet, observe ritual liturgies: the American Legion, the Boy Scouts, the Kiwanis, Rotary, and Lions clubs, etc. As far as I can determine, there are only two organizations in American society that include within their ritual liturgies a confession of sin. One is the church/synagogue. The other is Alcoholics Anonymous. When I was pastor of a church, I believed that one of our most serious

responsibilities in worship was to invite people to genuine honesty. I always, however, encountered members who urged, "Shouldn't we be upbeat in worship, making people feel better about themselves instead of worse? Is that prayer of confession necessary?" What do you think?

4. A young man named Chris Ashworth who grew up in our congregation formulated the following statement passed on to me by his father, Jack. "I carry my privilege like a piece of lumber, constantly worried I'll turn and hit someone with the half I can't see." Another church member, in a worship service, prayed, "Lord, forgive us for not wanting to get involved." See if you can identify genuine flaws that really matter in your life and articulate them. Don't settle for the banal: "I swear too much," or, "I'm not always nice." Skip the trite and search for the profound.

5. As I write these words, the Republican and Democratic party presidential nominating conventions are preparing to meet, both lauding Judeo-Christian (biblical) values. Can you imagine what would happen if either convention opened with a confession of sin?

6. A.A. meetings place confession at the center of everything they do. It is vitally important to them. Can you say exactly why, what they see is at stake? If you can't, find a friend who will tell you.

7. Our society has developed an entire vocabulary for diminishing one's own blame and deflecting it in other directions. Here are some of the terms we use. "Mistakes were made." "Collateral damage." "Unintended consequences." "Those words are no longer operative." "Disinformation." "Constructive ambiguity." Or, today's most popular term, "entry-level job," which often means, "I require a ton of hard work, pay the lowest wage I can get away with, and give no benefits." What terms can you add to this list? How do we mold language to avoid accountability?

8. I end with the following story.

One of my pastor colleagues arranged for a downtown hotel to provide lunch for a Jewish-Christian dialogue in which we were engaged. My colleague was meticulous in his plans: "Do not serve ham sandwiches! This is very important! Do you understand? Do not serve ham sandwiches!"

"We will serve only the meal you specify from our menu. If you don't want ham sandwiches, you do not have to worry." This reply came from the hotel's events manager.

"I don't need to be concerned with that?" my colleague said. "You assure me!"

"We assure you."

On the day of the lunch, wheeled through the kitchen door came—ham sandwiches. My colleague blew up. "NO HAM SAND-WICHES! You promised! Take them back! Take them back!" Our Jewish colleagues were moderately disgruntled, but more amused at my colleague's fervor—they knew him well and loved him. Twenty minutes later, we were all served chicken sandwiches.

After lunch, the confrontation occurred in the events manager's office. "Ma'am, you promised we would not be served ham sand-wiches! What happened?"

"Everything worked out okay, didn't it, sir?"

"If you call a drastic discourtesy and lunch twenty minutes late 'okay,' then, yes. Did you give my instruction to the kitchen? They told me they never heard anything about our menu choice."

"It all resolved, didn't it, sir? I think we ended up doing a pretty good job."

"But you promised me."

"We're terribly busy this time of year, sir. There was a mistake. It was quickly corrected. I don't know what more you can ask."

"You could have done what you promised."

"We do our best. When there is a problem, we try to fix it."

"Do you have anything else to say to me, ma'am?"

"No, I think I've said everything."

"Nothing at all?"

"You want me to apologize, don't you?"

"Yes, I do."

"That would be *weak*! We don't do the guilt thing around here."

In your experience, how typical is that of modern culture?

chapter eight

PSALMS 105, 106, AND 107

The Gospel according to Psalms

This marvelous little psalm cluster proclaims a mighty word, a gospel message that foreshadows the larger Bible. Embodied in it is a clear read on the human beings we are.

Psalm 105

"Remember the wonderful works (God) has done" this psalm proclaims, "his miracles, and the judgments he has uttered" (v. 5). This is the key line in Psalm 105, the point of the whole: remember! Remember how God raised us up from Abraham and Jacob (v. 6). Remember how God made a covenant with us and promised us the land (vv. 7-15). Remember how God acted against Egypt, our oppressors (vv. 16-25). Remember how God sent servant Moses (vv. 26-36). Remember how God brought us out of slavery in Egypt (vv. 37-43). Remember how God gave us the land (vv. 44-45). Remember!

There is a very unfortunate feature built into us human beings: we are really good at not remembering, at growing so accustomed to gracious gifts that we no longer notice them.

A short catalog of a few I have received. The huge crepe myrtle bush outside my window blazing pink and red. The hemlocks that form the backdrop. The safe, clean, sanitary house I am privileged to occupy. The land of freedom and opportunity in which I live.

Prosperity, "enough" for lots and lots of people. The capacity to stand, walk, lift, carry, and to think clearly. Enjoyable friends, fulfilling relationships. Family, children, grandchildren. Relative safety: I don't go to bed scared at night. Tasty and nutritious food. Clean, fresh water. Electricity. Light. Art. Books. All, gifts given. Yes, I may have had a hand in providing them, but fundamentally they were gifts.

Psalm 105 wants me to notice these things regularly and to remember where they came from. I have a strong tendency to get used to them, to turn them into "the way of life to which I have become accustomed," to presume.

Psalm 106

This psalm, in addition to being a national prayer of confession (as developed in the previous chapter), is pleading with God not to do what the humans do: forget. "Remember me, O LORD . . ." (v. 4). "They forgot . . ." says verse 21. They were "rebellious in their purposes, and were brought low through their iniquity" (v. 43). The psalm lays out a litany of iniquities Israel committed in their forgetfulness: we "rebelled against the Most High at the Red Sea" (v. 7), we "had a wanton craving in the wilderness, and put God to the test" (v. 14), we "made a calf at Horeb and worshiped a cast image" (v. 19), etc. But, "he remembered his covenant, and showed compassion according to the abundance of his steadfast love" (v. 45). The psalm ends by entreating God to be God, not human. Remember us! "Save us, O LORD our God, and gather us from among the nations . . ." (v. 47).

Psalm 107

107 O give thanks to the LORD, for he is good;
      for his steadfast love endures forever.
2 Let the redeemed of the LORD say so,
      those he redeemed from trouble
3 and gathered in from the lands,
      from the east and from the west,
      from the north and from the south.

4 Some wandered in desert wastes,
      finding no way to an inhabited town;
5 hungry and thirsty,
      their soul fainted within them.

6   Then they cried to the LORD in their trouble,
       and he delivered them from their distress;
7   he led them by a straight way,
       until they reached an inhabited town.
8   Let them thank the LORD for his steadfast love,
       for his wonderful works to humankind.
9   For he satisfies the thirsty,
       and the hungry he fills with good things.

10 Some sat in darkness and in gloom,
       prisoners in misery and in irons,
11 for they had rebelled against the words of God,
       and spurned the counsel of the Most High.
12 Their hearts were bowed down with hard labor;
       they fell down with no one to help.
13 Then they cried to the LORD in their trouble,
       and he saved them from their distress;
14 he brought them out of darkness and gloom,
       and broke their bonds asunder.
15 Let them thank the LORD for his steadfast love,
       for his wonderful works to humankind.
16 For he shatters the doors of bronze,
       and cuts in two the bars of iron.

17 Some were sick through their sinful ways,
       and because of their iniquities endured affliction;
18 they loathed any kind of food,
       and they drew near to the gates of death.
19 Then they cried to the LORD in their trouble,
       and he saved them from their distress;
20 he sent out his word and healed them,
       and delivered them from destruction.
21 Let them thank the LORD for his steadfast love,
       for his wonderful works to humankind.
22 And let them offer thanksgiving sacrifices,
       and tell of his deeds with songs of joy.

23 Some went down to the sea in ships,
       doing business on the mighty waters;
24 they saw the deeds of the LORD,
       his wondrous works in the deep.
25 For he commanded and raised up the stormy wind,
       which lifted up the waves of the sea.

26 They mounted up to heaven, they went down to the depths;
  their courage melted away in their calamity;
27 they reeled and staggered like drunkards,
  and were at their wits' end.
28 Then they cried to the LORD in their trouble,
  and he brought them out from their distress;
29 he made the storm be still,
  and the waves of the sea were hushed.
30 Then they were glad because they had quiet,
  and he brought them to their desired haven.
31 Let them thank the LORD for his steadfast love,
  for his wonderful works to humankind.
32 Let them extol him in the congregation of the people,
  and praise him in the assembly of the elders.

33 He turns rivers into a desert,
  springs of water into thirsty ground,
34 a fruitful land into a salty waste,
  because of the wickedness of its inhabitants.
35 He turns the desert into pools of water,
  a parched land into springs of water.
36 And there he lets the hungry live,
  and they establish a town to live in;
37 they sow fields, and plant vineyards,
  and get a fruitful yield.
38 By his blessing they multiply greatly,
  and he does not let their cattle decrease.

39 When they are diminished and brought low
  through oppression, trouble, and sorrow,
40 he pours contempt on princes
  and makes them wander in trackless wastes;
41 but he raises up the needy out of distress,
  and makes their families like flocks.
42 The upright see it and are glad;
  and all wickedness stops its mouth.
43 Let those who are wise give heed to these things,
  and consider the steadfast love of the LORD.

Psalm 107 has one subject: God's steadfast love.

The psalm begins (vv. 1-3) with a call to thanksgiving from all the beneficiaries, those whom God has redeemed from every corner of the earth.

A special note is due on the word "redeem," used in verse 2, especially since it is a concept used prolifically as the Bible moves forward. If, in ancient Israel, a person became destitute, too poor to survive, that person might sell himself into slavery, trading labor for sustenance. If this happened, it was the obligation as the next-of-kin to buy the person back out of slavery. This was called "redeeming." It was a profoundly embedded concept in the Israelite mind. Since God redeemed us when we were slaves in Egypt, we are to do what God has done, redeeming one another.

Psalm 107 shows four episodes of redemption. In verses 4-9, some people were lost in a desert, unable to find their way. They cried out to God for help. God led them to safety, for which they are bidden to give thanks for God's redeeming steadfast love.

Verses 10-16 present people imprisoned "in darkness and in gloom, prisoners in misery and in irons" (v. 10). They cried out to God for help. God led them to freedom, for which they are bidden to give thanks for God's redeeming steadfast love.

In verses 17-22, people were sick, "loathing any kind of food, drawing near to the gates of death" (v. 19). They cried out to God for help. God healed them, delivering them from destruction, for which they are bidden to give thanks for God's redeeming steadfast love.

Verses 23-32 present ship travelers who encountered a great storm at sea. "They mounted up to heaven, and they sank to the depths; their courage melted away" (v. 26). They cried out to God for help. God made the storm be still and hushed the waves, for which they are bidden to give thanks for God's redeeming steadfast love.

Verses 33-38 recite redeeming acts of many kinds. And verses 39-42 declare God's strong empathy for the needy and the diminished. The psalm ends (v. 43) with the admonition, "Let those who are wise give heed to these things, and consider the steadfast love of the LORD."

Psalm 107 presents a new face of God's compassion. Elsewhere, it has been an empowering strength in battle or a shield and protector against danger. In Psalm 107, God's love becomes a pursuing force that seeks to find us in the places of our desolation, a persistent searcher tracking us in our exiles. The psalm's energy implies that the searcher is not to be denied!

The Psalm 105, 106, and 107 Cluster

This three-psalm cluster presents what may be the most fundamental theological message in the entire book, what we might call "the gospel according to Psalms." The word "gospel" in Greek means "good news," and the message spoken is most certainly that. The cluster also speaks to what has been an enormous theological dilemma in the Jewish/Christian tradition through the years: God's relation to bad things that happen.

Following the beautiful present-tense creation story of Psalm 104, a story of unending gifts given by God through the natural world, this psalm cluster presents three scenes.

Psalm 105 shows gifts given to Israel in particular: the covenant made with Abraham; deliverance at the Red Sea; Moses' leadership; and the gift of the Promised Land. The *remember!* admonition actually applies to both Psalms 104 and 105. The key ingredient in remembering is: living with hearts of thanks! (Both the Passover ritual of Judaism and the sacramental supper of Christianity focus on motivating the faithful to remember.)

Psalm 106 is a portrait of Israel's not remembering. They turned to iniquity and wickedness. Thus was God's great anger kindled. God abhorred Israel (v. 40), and gave them into the hands of foreigners who subjected and oppressed them (v. 42). Many times did God deliver them, but Israel persisted in not remembering (v. 43). The final word in this psalm is a fervent plea, "Save us, O LORD our God, and gather us from among the nations" (v. 47).

Psalm 107 depicts four metaphors of the oppression to which Israel fell victim. In each case, "they cried to the LORD in their trouble" (v. 6) and the steadfast love of God heard them, reached forth, and rescued them. With each episode, we are bidden to "thank the LORD for his steadfast love" (v. 8), the underlying theme.

The cluster's point is that God, out of love, gives gifts; Israel forgets and suffers mightily, finally crying out; God, out of love, reclaims. This is the editors' fundamental picture of the God-human dynamic. The pattern is stated succinctly in Psalm 106:43.

Many times he delivered them,
>   but they were rebellious in their purposes,
>   and were brought low through their iniquity.
Nevertheless he regarded their distress
>   when he heard their cry.

The remarkable feature of the editors' pattern is that there is one constant throughout the story: God's love. Steadfast, indeed! The gifts come from love, the concluding redemption is motivated by love, and we suddenly realize that God's love remains through our rebelliousness. God's love, in other words, accompanies God's wrath. Great compassion and great anger reside in the same Deity at the same time, even though that may be a logical contradiction. No explanation is provided; the fact is simply stated.

We moderns turn this into a very large philosophical problem: How can a loving God allow (even, perhaps, inflict) tragedy? Why doesn't the all-compassionate Lord prevent our rebelliousness and spare us our consequences? The Psalms editors were not bothered by the contradiction. Life happens this way, and it is from life, not from logic, that we take our theology. We believe things about God because we experience them, not because we logically reason them. Psalm theology was "experiential theology."

This God-dynamic occurs prolifically among humans. Is it not perfectly possible for a parent to love a child profoundly, to the depths, but also to get exceedingly upset and angry, even to punish? Can not this be very good parenting? Hosea 11:1-9 tells this story graphically with God as the parent and Israel as the child.

Thus do we see "the gospel according to Psalms" in the 105–107 cluster: that through the worst rebellions we human beings concoct, the steadfast love of God persists—and finally triumphs. In the words of a later interpreter, "For I am convinced that neither death, nor life, nor angels, nor rulers, nor things present, nor things to come, nor powers, nor height, nor depth, nor anything else in all creation, will be able to separate us (that is, to keep us separated) from the love of God in Christ Jesus our LORD" (Rom 8:38-39).

Discussion Topics and Questions

1. What are things you too easily forget and lose sight of, gifts that would make you a considerably more thankful person if you kept them in mind? List several. What might create a less forgetful you and me?

2. If you were adding a strophe to Psalm 107, an instance in which people you know of (maybe you, yourself) were in extreme trouble and were redeemed by God's steadfast love, how would it go?

3. Can you describe a human instance in which you have seen great love and great anger both present in one person at the same time? What happened?

4. Human development specialists say that *basic trust*, a fundamental belief that those around me love me and are to be trusted, is probably the most vital item that can be implanted in any human being, conveyed through a mother and a father in one's earliest months. They also say that a child raised without rigorous expectations is a child deprived. Unconditional love and serious expectations: Have you seen both of these exercised effectively at the same time?

chapter nine
EXODUS 32–34, PSALM 103, NAHUM, AND JONAH

God Forgives: Blessing and Challenge

Some psalms carry on conversation with biblical texts outside the book. Psalm 103 is an example of one of the most vital. The conversation involves a deep and primitive struggle that goes on forever in you and me.

Exodus 32–34

The book of Exodus begins with Israel a slave nation in Egypt. With Moses as their leader, God delivered Israel to freedom by parting the waters of the Red Sea. Exodus 15 records Israel's song of joyous thanksgiving sung and danced on the eastern bank.

They proceeded down the Sinai Peninsula toward Mount Sinai. Arriving, Moses ascended the mountain to receive the Ten Commandments and the covenant code, God's instructions on how the nation was to live its life. While Moses was atop Sinai, however, Israel rebelled, casting a golden calf to worship rather than God (Exod 32–34). God saw this and became enraged, killing numbers of Israelites and vowing to abandon the others. Moses, however, pleaded mightily for God's mercy. God finally repented, deciding not to destroy Israel after all but to forgive them. Thus did God speak before Moses:

> The Lord, the Lord,
>   a God merciful and gracious,
>   slow to anger,
>   and abounding in steadfast love and faithfulness . . .
>   (Exod 34:6)

From this moment forward, Israel's Mount Sinai experience would stand as a memorial not only to the giving of the law but also to *God's willingness to grant pardon*. Here, this remarkable and absolutely astounding characteristic of God was most clearly revealed: God's forgiveness. Israel would have been annihilated without it! There would have been no further story! Israel would remember and reflect on God's incredible forgiveness through generations to come.

As we proceed now, lock into your mind the words quoted above: ". . . a God merciful and gracious, slow to anger, and abounding in steadfast love and faithfulness." They are what we might call "footnote words." Every time they or some portion of them appears elsewhere in Scripture, they are meant to take us—our minds and memories—back to Mount Sinai to the wondrous and magnificent day when God forgave Israel rather than destroying it.

Psalm 103

103 Bless the Lord, O my soul,
         and all that is within me,
         bless his holy name.
2   Bless the Lord, O my soul,
         and do not forget all his benefits—
3   who forgives all your iniquity,
         who heals all your diseases,
4   who redeems your life from the Pit,
         who crowns you with steadfast love and mercy,
5   who satisfies you with good as long as you live
         so that your youth is renewed like the eagle's.

6   The Lord works vindication
         and justice for all who are oppressed.

7   He made known his ways to Moses,
     his acts to the people of Israel.
8   The LORD is merciful and gracious,
     slow to anger and abounding in steadfast love.
9   He will not always accuse,
     nor will he keep his anger forever.
10   He does not deal with us according to our sins,
     nor repay us according to our iniquities.
11   For as the heavens are high above the earth,
     so great is his steadfast love toward those who fear him;
12   as far as the east is from the west,
     so far he removes our transgressions from us.
13   As a father has compassion on his children,
     so the LORD has compassion for those who fear him.
14   For he knows how we are made;
     he remembers that we are dust.

15   As for mortals, their days are like grass;
     they flourish like a flower of the field;
16   for the wind passes over it, and it is gone,
     and its place knows it no more.
17   But the steadfast love of the LORD is from everlasting to
     everlasting,
     on those who fear him,
     and his righteousness to children's children,
18   to those who keep his covenant
     and remember to do his commandments.

19   The LORD has established his throne in the heavens,
     and his kingdom rules over all.
20   Bless the LORD, O you his angels,
     you mighty ones who do his bidding,
     obedient to his spoken word.
21   Bless the LORD, all his hosts,
     his ministers that do his will.
22   Bless the LORD, all his works,
     in all places of his dominion.
     Bless the LORD, O my soul.

Psalm 103 is a celebration of the day God forgave Israel at Sinai! We do not know the exact setting in which the psalm was used, but there is no mistaking the cause of the celebration.

Verses 1-5 present a call for everyone to bless the Lord from deep in the heart: "Bless the LORD, O my soul!"

Verses 6-7 are highly significant, though they may not seem so at first.

> The LORD works vindication
>> and justice for all who are oppressed.
> He made known his ways to Moses,
>> his acts to the people of Israel.

This is a reference to God's appearance in Egypt to deliver Israel from slavery. That deliverance is called "justice," *mispat* in Hebrew. *Mispat* is a concept used prolifically by the Old Testament prophets and in the Psalms. Amos declared, "Let justice roll down like waters" (5:24). "Give the king your justice, O God," petitions Psalm 72:1. Calls for justice have sounded across our own generation as well, racial justice, gender justice, economic justice, and others, often using Amos' highly memorable words.

We moderns often think of "justice" as "being fair," treating everyone the same, as we say, "creating a level playing field." That is not at all what the Bible means by "justice." Biblical justice is precisely what is stated in Psalm 103:6-7. It is doing what God did in Egypt, working "vindication . . . for all who are oppressed," delivering slaves from their slavery, the afflicted from their afflictions. "Justice" is tilting the playing field so that the powerless can gain strength and survive. This is not the main subject of Psalm 103, but it is a significant point.

Verses 8-14 arrive at the psalm's major subject. Note the beginning words, "The LORD is merciful and gracious, slow to anger and abounding in steadfast love" (v. 8). The words are a direct quote from Exodus 34, a footnote, meaning that the psalm bids us to bring to mind the golden calf story, particularly how God's forgiveness occurred in that story.

Verses 9-14 are the psalmist's primary declaration. They declare that God forgets! Forgets the wretched garbage we do. Forgets our golden calves, our rebellions. Forgets our complaining and our criticisms. God may be very angry for a while, but God "gets over it." God does not keep a huge record book of our iniquities and hold them against us through eternity. God forgets.

In this regard God is not like us humans. We can remember forever, slights big and small, ills performed, hurts that have wounded. We remember and don't let go. We can maintain unending grudges. God, thank God, isn't like us, Psalm 103 is saying. "As the heavens are high above the earth" (v. 11), ". . . as far as the east is from the west, so far he removes our transgressions from us" (v. 12). "As a father has compassion on his children, so the LORD has compassion on those who fear him" (v. 13).

The psalm then goes on to talk about how brief and fragile we are, limited creatures hardly capable of reflecting God. But this is to contrast God's steadfast love with us, "from everlasting to everlasting" (v. 17), a forgiveness knowing no end.

Psalm 103 is a massive celebration of God's forgiving nature! At Mount Sinai, we would not have survived, we would have been corpses on the wilderness floor, if God had not been forgiving. "He does not deal with us according to our sins, nor repay us according to our iniquities" (v. 10). "The LORD is merciful and gracious, slow to anger and abounding in steadfast love" (v. 8). Thus does the psalm sing.

We do not have any idea of who formulated Psalm 103 or when, but it obviously was attached to some worship ritual celebrating God's forgiving, forgetful heart.

Nahum

The last half of the eighth century BCE was what Dr. James Sanders called "the first holocaust of the Jews." From shortly after 740 to around 698, Israel was subjected to repeated military barrages from the most feared and hated enemy their world had ever known, the mighty Assyrians. Assyria—centered in Nineveh on the Tigris River (in current day Iraq)—was a giant, brutal invader, respecting no one else's territory or property, no one else's culture, no one else's religion, no one else's life. Assyria invaded for one purpose only: to loot, desecrate, humiliate, and destroy. Their artists, seeking to regale in the nation's power and brutality, left numerous large stone carvings showing massive numbers of Assyrian army troops ripping down protective walls and overwhelming cities, carvings that now reside in various historical museums around the world. Archeology tells us that in one Israelite town the Assyrians murdered all the residents, piled their bodies in a huge pit, and covered them with pig bones, remnants from the army's evening meal—a testimony to Assyrian disdain.

This half century of brutal onslaughts (at least four of them) ensconced Assyria/Nineveh as the epitome of hell itself in the Israelite mind, evil and iniquity incarnate. Rage, fury, and hatred against Nineveh and their marauding kings would persist long after Assyria was defeated by the Babylonians in 618 BCE. Nineveh became the metaphorical symbol of any outsider who invaded and plundered Israel, whether it was Babylon, Persia, Greece, or Rome. All were labeled "Nineveh."

Nahum's prophecy is a blistering condemnation of Nineveh. "A jealous and avenging God is the LORD," it begins, "the LORD is avenging and wrathful; the LORD takes vengeance on his adversaries and rages against his enemies" (1:2).

The key statement in the entire book comes in verse 3a: "The LORD is slow to anger . . ." This easy-to-miss comment is, as we know now, a quote from Exodus 34:6. Nahum quotes as little of the verse as possible while still noting it. The translation might better be rendered: "Yes, I know that the Lord is slow to anger, (abounding in steadfast love) . . . *but* . . . !" Nahum knows fully God's reputation for forgiving, but wants quickly to set that aside and get on with the vital matter at hand: condemning Nineveh! "(God is also) great in power, and the LORD will by no means clear the guilty!" (v. 3b). Nineveh has been so despicable, so loathsome, that forgiveness doesn't even come up. Through the remainder of the book, Nahum seethes vengeance.

Chapter 2 describes God's "shatterer," the army of ravagers that invade the evil city, its warriors clothed in crimson as their chariots race madly through the streets. "Plunder the silver! Plunder the gold!" the cry goes out. Hearts are faint and Nineveh's knees tremble!

"Ah! City of bloodshed," continues chapter 3, "utterly deceitful, full of booty . . . , I am against you, says the LORD of hosts . . . . I will throw filth at you, and treat you with contempt, and make you a spectacle . . . . The fire will devour you, the sword will cut you off. . . . For who has ever escaped your endless cruelty?"

Nahum prophesies retribution unqualified, reprisal without pity. Vanquish talk of pardon. Dance and celebrate with Psalm 103 all you wish, but the cold, brutal fact is that Nineveh has been the scourge of Nahum's world for over two hundred years, and now he intends to pay it its full due from a wrathful God who remembers everything and forgives nothing. And Nahum cannot wait to watch it happen! "Devastation, desolation, and destruction!" (2:10). With that, alone, will God be content! The word of the prophet, Nahum!

Jonah

Jonah, the prophet, shares Nahum's scorn for Nineveh, but the book of Jonah is quite a different matter. Whereas Nahum was a prophetic diatribe declared by Nahum himself, the book of Jonah is a highly imaginative story told by a narrator, and the narrator's mind goes a very different direction. The book ends not with a declaration but with a question mark, one that reaches across centuries, posed to you and me and all other believers.

Jonah, the story goes, was a prophet in Jerusalem, one vested with the responsibility of delivering the word of God to earth. God spoke to Jonah (chapter 1) and said: Jonah, stand on your feet and go at once to Nineveh, that great city of the Assyrians, and cry out against it, for the wickedness of that city—the devastation it has wrought on many peoples—has become an abomination before me.

Jonah stood on his feet, but instead of journeying eastward toward Nineveh, he turned westward toward the Mediterranean seaport town of Joppa, near current day Tel Aviv. He did this, the story says, to escape the presence of the Lord. And as if Joppa were not far enough from the presence of the Lord, Jonah bought a ticket on a boat headed toward Tarshish, 350 miles north in present-day Turkey.

Please understand that Jonah was not fleeing because he was scared to go to the great evil city. Personal fear had nothing to do with it. His reason will emerge.

As the boat sailed up the Mediterranean coast, God, not at all pleased with what was developing, hurled a great wind upon the sea. The rickety ship rolled up and down, side to side, to the heights and to the depths, threatening to break up. Even the veteran sailors were terrified. Each cried out to his god for mercy and help, but the storm did not abate. They ran this way and that across the deck, seeking some incantation, some ritual formula that would quiet the wind, but nothing worked.

The sailors finally decided to cast lots to see if someone on the boat had committed some evil for which they were all being punished. The lot, of course, fell on Jonah, and he confessed: Yes, I am your problem, he said. I am Jonah, a Hebrew from Israel. I worship the Lord, the God of heaven, who made the sea and the dry land. I am, in fact, a prophet, a spokesman dedicated to God's service. But I am here fleeing from God's presence, for I very much no not want to do what God has assigned to me. Throw me into the sea, and the storm will stop.

The sailors reluctantly did so, tossing Jonah overboard. As soon as he sank under the water, the storm did stop, and there was what the Gospel of Mark (4:39) will later call "a dead calm." Whereupon the sailors feared Jonah's God exceedingly!

As Jonah sank under the water, he was swallowed by a large fish (the story doesn't say "whale"; it says "large fish"). Jonah spent three days and three nights in the belly of the fish, pondering his fate. When he finally decided that it was time to call upon God once more, Jonah sang a little song that he had learned in Saturday school (chapter 2). The song talked about how God hears people who call from the depths of Sheol and reaches forth to save them. It ended with the singer vowing that if God would just save him on this one occasion, Jonah would double his church pledge and pay it all off the following Sabbath. (I think I've heard that line somewhere before.)

Apparently, God liked the song, because God spoke to the fish, and the fish gave out one huge upchuck and deposited Jonah on the beach. It was a scene so incredible that even Cecil B. DeMille did not try to re-create it on film.

As Jonah sat drying off, the word of God came to him again, "Jonah, stand on your feet and go immediately to Nineveh, that great city of the Assyrians, and cry out against it!" This time, Jonah went.

When he got to Nineveh, he found a city fifty miles in breadth, incredible even now, unheard of in ancient times—used in the story to amplify how huge and powerful the great hated tyrant was. Jonah went in, located a street corner, stood on a crate, and declared: Forty days and Nineveh will be destroyed for all its murderous wickedness! That was his entire sermon.

But—behold!—and this is where the story reaches its most imaginative heights—Nineveh repented! The people proclaimed a fast and put on sackcloth, the ancient mode of showing repentance. They begged God to forgive them for all their evil among the nations. The king of Nineveh heard of it, he vacated his throne, removed his purple robe, covered himself with sackcloth, and sat in ashes—national repentance.

When God saw that Nineveh was repenting, God also repented of the destruction God had intended to do against the city, deciding not to punish it after all. This made Jonah angry as a scorched hornet's nest, or, as the staid, flat New Revised Standard Version of the Bible, which excels in understatement, puts it, he was "exceedingly displeased." And he bawled at God: I knew you were going to do this, God! You're nothing but a soft touch! This is why I didn't want to come to this wretched city in the first place, because I knew that if they heeded my preaching and repented, you would forgive them! 'Slow to anger, and abounding in steadfast love' (Jonah 4:2): they sure got that one right about you! Don't let these dirty, nasty, arrogant people get away with what they've done! Burn'um! Clean'um out! Destroy them! Pay them back in full measure for the way they've treated the rest of us! To forgive these low-life wretches is an international disgrace against your name!

Jonah stalked out of the city and settled himself at a distance under a bush, waiting to see if God wouldn't have a change of mind and burn the place after all. But God finally declared, "Jonah, why should I not pity Nineveh, that great city in which there more than 120,000 people who do not know their right hands from their left" (that is, who have repented from their evil), and then the enigmatic words on which the book of Jonah ends, "and also much cattle." Does that mean that Nineveh's cows repented also?

Jonah joins Nahum in being aware of God's profoundly forgiving heart, as illustrated at Sinai. But, whereas Nahum quickly sets it aside and makes God a figure of anger and battle fury, Jonah knows from the beginning that this forgiving feature of God will prevail. The last thing he wants to do is carry out his prophetic assignment and see it happen. Which it does.

The story writer of Jonah is delivering a different message altogether. It's wonderful, the writer is saying, it is magnificent, it is exhilarating when God forgives *us*. Let us dance and sing and worship joyously, proclaiming Psalm 103 with full voice! But it becomes entirely different when God forgives *them*, our mortal enemy! God is one hundred percent and completely not supposed to do that! God has to share our disdain, our hatred, our unforgiving anger! If we detest Assyrians, God is supposed to detest Assyrians too! If we loathe terrorists, God is supposed to loathe terrorists. To be a worthwhile god at all, God has to confirm our deepest emotions! When it comes down to the hard realities and the bitter disputes of life, God must be on our side! Anything less is intolerable!

The point of the Jonah story is that God does things God's own way. God can forgive Nineveh. God can forgive Rome, the giant nemesis in Jesus' day. God can forgive Germany, Japan. God can forgive Russia, North Korea, North Vietnam. God can forgive basketball players who play for Duke (I lived in Kentucky for thirty years). God can forgive Republicans or Democrats, whichever one you aren't. God can forgive them because God loves them. The hardest challenge in the faith you and I profess is to believe profoundly and sincerely that we, human beings, are all brothers and sisters, children of Adam and Eve, and that God loves *them* just as much as God loves *us*.

Some years ago I attended a lecture on Jonah by Jewish scholar Yitz Greenberg held at the Jewish Community Center in Louisville, Kentucky. Rabbi Greenberg carried us through the Jonah story much as I have here, except that he was a linguistic scholar, which I am not. At the close of his presentation, Rabbi Greenberg said to the packed, hushed convocation, "After reading Jonah, I have to ask myself honestly: Is this book in my Holy Bible saying to me that God may feel differently from the way I do about—Adolph Hitler?" With that, the Rabbi sat down, leaving all present in stunned silence. That is the question.

Discussion Topics and Questions

1. Formulate exactly what you think Rabbi Greenberg was and was not saying.

2. The last time I preached on Psalm 103, I entitled the sermon, "God Forgets." The sermon message could be stated in two words:

"Can we?" One sentence from the sermon was, "When I counsel a couple getting married, we always talk about forgetting, because in every good marriage, there's going to be a lot of forgetting to do." Not necessarily resolving, but leaving behind. Compare that with your experience.

3. See if the following story resonates with anything in you.

I recall vividly the first time I ever heard truly foul, filthy language coming from adults. I was about eleven years old—old enough that on summer nights my friends and I were allowed to play across the neighborhood with flashlights. On this particular night, Clint Butler and I had found some chalk, and we were drawing pictures of our schoolteachers on the sidewalk in front of his house. I was drawing my fifth-grade teacher, Mrs. Yost, a tall, vigorous, big-boned woman who seemed to smother our classroom and our lives with her imposing presence. Clint was drawing "the witch woman," a lady who stood at the cafeteria door every lunch and made us eat all our food before we could leave. It was "the witch woman" who had first taught us that line about "all the hungry children in China."

Clint's father appeared behind us, ambling peacefully, out for an evening stroll. He commented innocently, "What are you boys up to?" I don't remember what we said. What I remember is that, suddenly, without warning, an incredible burst of profanity blasted from across the street, language so bad that I didn't even know what half of it meant. It was Mr. Copple who had built a house across the street from the Butlers and moved in two weeks earlier. He was aiming his nasty words at Mr. Butler.

Butler, coming to life immediately, fired his own salvo back at Copple. Copple returned the insult with triple vengeance. Butler was fully up to the challenge. By this time, they were both seething snake venom. Copple proclaimed Butler doomed in the afterlife. Butler accused Copple of Freudian incest. Copple insulted Butler's parentage. Butler equated Copple with the equine posterior. Before it ended, I thought we were going to have a full-scale brawl right in the middle of Melrose Street.

I would learn later that this was normal behavior between these two. When they ran into each other on the street, when they saw each other across the block, they never missed an opportunity. On a pleasant summer afternoon in our neighborhood, you would suddenly hear a vulgar blast of profanity igniting the atmosphere, and you would know that Copple and Butler were walking their dogs.

"How did it begin?" I asked Clint.

"Ole man Copple insulted my Dad," Clint replied, "called him a liar."

"What were they arguing about?" I asked.

"I don't know," Clint answered, "it happened before I was born."

One insult twelve years previously, and neither of them had ever forgotten! I think they had come to need each other.

4. "For my thoughts are not your thoughts, nor are your ways my ways, says the LORD. For as the heavens are higher than the earth, so are my ways higher than your ways and my thoughts than your thoughts" (Isa 55:8-9). Repeatedly throughout the Bible, as in this scene from second Isaiah, the vast, immense difference between God and us is illustrated by God's capacity and our incapacity to forgive. (Matthew plays the same theme in 18:21-35.) You and I have an enormous struggle forgiving people who have wronged us deeply. Wrongs against us can plague us for years, causing much more harm to us than to those who wronged us. As the texts cited above indicate, God handles forgiveness very differently. I think we do not have the wisdom to understand. But, would you agree that, beneath it all, our call is to do what God has done?

chapter ten

PSALMS 118 AND 96–100, ISAIAH 40, AND THE NEW TESTAMENT

Coronation Procession

Psalms 96–100 and Psalm 118 take their place in a much larger biblical picture that I want to develop with you in this final study chapter. The four gospel writers have used this larger picture to provide the structure for their books. Isaiah 40 and Philippians 2 are also related. I find the picture quite astounding, clarifying things that were previously obscure. I hope you find it the same way. We begin with background.

Ancient Coronation Processions

In the ancient Far East and Middle East, a ritual practice shared by many, many cultures was the *coronation procession*, a community event for the crowning of a king. We, today, observe such a ritual when, as part of a presidential inauguration, we include a motorcade down Pennsylvania Avenue in Washington, DC. Coronation processions in ancient times tended to be extravagantly elaborate, great shows of self-proclamation and hubris. Throngs turned out, whole communities, lining the procession route, shouting, singing, chanting, celebrating (just as we line Pennsylvania Avenue). The ancient processions took quite different forms in different places.

Google "ancient coronation processions" for examples. From all the diversity, five procession elements seem to emerge as most common.

The announcer. The coronation procession was led by an announcer at the head, proclaiming what was happening. "Prepare yourselves! Fall to your knees! The king comes! The great and mighty one; chosen of the gods! Let all bow in humble reverence!" This was the essence of the announcement, said in many different forms and ways. The announcer might be accompanied by trumpets, by stringed instruments, by dancers, by chanters, by anything that would call the throngs to attention. To provide a carpet for the king, the crowd might spread garments or leafy branches on the processional path.

The evidences. Following the announcer was a display of evidences meant to prove that the gods endorsed and supported this king. The proofs were usually booty from successful military conquests, indicators that the gods had given this king victory and were with him. Jewels, gold, ornaments, swords, shields, chariots—they might all be on display, whatever the king's men had seized from defeated enemies. The larger the display, the more convincing the case. Great mounds of evidence might be exhibited.

The king riding. Most prominently displayed was the king-to-be-crowned riding some sort of vehicle. It might be a chair carried on horizontal poles. It might be a royal wagon drawn by animals. It might be an elephant, a horse, a camel, or a donkey. The regal adornment of king and vehicle would reach a peak of splendor, designed to leave all viewing the procession in breathless awe.

The king's crown. The path of the procession would lead to some religious site—a temple or an altar or a shrine—where, in the name of the gods, a crown would be placed upon the king's head by a priest. The king would also be robed in a purple garment, the color of kings.

The king's throne. The procession would finally deliver the king to his royal throne, high and lifted up, which he would ascend in regal magnificence.

From allusions dotted through the Bible, it seems that ancient Israel practiced its own versions of this coronation procession across hundreds of years. In some eras it may have been a yearly festival;

in others only when a new king ascended the throne. But over those centuries the coronation procession became deeply, deeply engraved in Israelite minds. It was a peak moment for everyone, a happening to be remembered and told of across generations: the moment when God acted to send a new "anointed one" to lead God's people.

Israel's version of the coronation procession seems to have proceeded as follows. The procession originated outside the walls of the city, some distance down the Jericho road, east of Jerusalem. The Jericho road, beginning to end, was a thirty-five-hundred-foot uphill climb from the Jordan River valley to the top of Mount Zion. The coronation procession would have covered only a small distance of the upper portion, but it would still have been an uphill trek. The location of the starting place would have conveyed two meanings.

In Israel's thought-world, "east" symbolized new beginnings, promise. The sun arose in the east. Each new day began there and spread across the sky. Announcements from God (a brightly shining star) and gifts from God (gold, frankincense, and myrrh) came from the east, symbolizing promise and hope.

And, further, to have the procession start some distance down the hill signified humble beginnings. Israel nourished in its heart the belief that God's way was to begin with the small, the obscure, the powerless, the disregarded, and create greatness. God could take a tiny mustard seed and make from it a great, thriving plant. God could take a stone the builders rejected as inferior and make from it the chief cornerstone of a vast structure. God could take a tiny, imperiled slave community in Egypt and form it into a nation more numerous than the stars in the sky or the grains of sand on the seashore. God could take a small, young boy with a rock and sling and empower him to slay the mighty Philistine Goliath, and thence become Israel's greatest king. This was God's way. For the Israelite coronation procession to begin below the crest of the hill, in a place of humility, and ascend toward the city was God's way of doing things.

This pattern, this theology, was not common across their ancient world. Most kings wanted to portray themselves as power figures from the start, invincible sons of divinities. Imperial direction was their way, most certainly not humility. Israel arrived at its very different theology from its exodus beginnings. When God visited Egypt, Israel understood, God came to collude not with Pharaoh on how to rule but with Pharaoh's slaves on how to escape. God took up residence in the huts and hovels of Egypt, not in the royal palace. This notion of humble beginnings shaped Israelite faith comprehensively and for centuries.

Amid celebration by the attending crowd, the Israelite coronation procession would proceed up the hill toward Jerusalem's gate. The celebration would be enormous—shouting, singing, chanting, instruments playing, dancing. People would lay garments and leafy branches on the road to cushion the procession's path. The uproar would be so intense, so captivating, that it would be easy to get the feeling that the entire creation was joining in: the trees dancing, the hills singing, the waves on the distant seashore clapping their hands, even the rocks by the side of the road shouting their acclaim! It seemed that people from near and far beheld the splendor, nations witnessing the spectacle. The whole earth, the whole creation, joined the festivity on this magical day.

I remember well the first downtown parade I ever attended. It was a Christmas parade along Fourth Street in Winston-Salem, North Carolina, my hometown. I was six or seven years old. The floats came by, each wondrous, magical. The town's three high schools bands marched. The horse riders, the motorcycles, the unicycles, the jugglers, the clowns, the street performers. And Santa riding his sleigh pulled by reindeer. I was captured by the moment. In my mind the whole world was focused here. Can you remember similar parade times?

Approaching the Jerusalem gate, the procession would engage in some sort of liturgy for gaining entrance, scripted words spoken back and forth between procession members and gatekeepers. With the gate opening, the procession would move forward into the city streets amid great uproar and celebration. The entourage would proceed to the Temple, where a crown would be placed on the king's head by a priest, and subsequently the king would ascend his royal throne.

Why No Detailed Record?

This picture of the Israelite coronation procession has been patched together from several passages in the Bible. No single text gives the entire story. Because of this, the portrait drawn above remains provisional, the best one can do. The character of Israel's coronation processions developed over a thousand-year period, so large variations would have occurred. But the fundamental point here is that *however it happened*, the coronation procession left an indelible mark on the Israelite mind. From generation to generation, everybody knew about it, recognized its contours, and shared the hope and expectation enlivened by it!

Why, then, is there not in Scripture a full description? Why only bits of allusion?

I ask you to step back with me for a moment and play a little game. Get rid of what we have been talking about here, and settle your mind in this present moment. We'll return to coronation processions shortly.

I want to speak to you a simple sentence, and I want you to roll that sentence over in your mind, uncovering the many things you know that are buried in it. The sentence is this:

> The children emerged from the basement playroom to find a cake with six pink candles on the dining room table.

That's all you get, that one simple sentence. But think now beyond those few words. What else does the sentence tell you? Name additional things *you know* are going on in this scene, additional statements you could add with reasonable certainty. Let me get you started.

> We are at a child's birthday party.
> The children were playing party games in the basement playroom.
> One game they played was "pin the tail on the donkey."
> The birthday kid is a girl.
> Six years old.

That gets you started? Keep going.

> The children will now gather around the dining room table.
> An adult will light the candles.
> The whole gathering will sing "Happy Birthday!" to the tune everyone knows.
> The birthday girl will close her eyes, make a wish, and then try to blow out all the candles in one puff.
> Pieces of cake will be cut, set on plates, and given to each child.

Some adult will come around adding a dip of ice cream to the
cake plates.
The birthday girl will then open presents brought by her
friends.

All of these things you, yourself, could readily have added to the
one sentence above; is that not true? And why is it you could do
that? It's simple: *because you have been there*, ten times, twenty
times, thirty times. You and others around you know the customs
by personal experience. If a family from Mongolia moved in next
door to you and came over to inquire, "Where can we read of
American child birthday customs? Tell us some book that will explain them?" where would you send them? Has anyone ever written
all this down? Even on the internet? No. And why not? Because
everyone knows it already! It would be superfluous, redundant,
boring. Nobody would be interested.

This illustrates a remarkable, sometimes challenging quality of
biblical literature: the writers don't tell us what they think everyone
already knows. They tend to be minimalists, not overtelling. Many
times they just drop in a word or two, a sentence, to bring forward
into our minds a full picture they believe is already there.

Sometimes this leads to a difficult chase for those of us who live
two and three thousand years later. Sometimes we have to collect
bits and pieces and construct pictures of the things everyone back
then knew about, like coronation processions.

Psalm 118

118 O give thanks to the LORD, for he is good;
    his steadfast love endures forever!

2   Let Israel say,
        "His steadfast love endures forever."
3   Let the house of Aaron say,
        "His steadfast love endures forever."
4   Let those who fear the LORD say,
        "His steadfast love endures forever."

5   Out of my distress I called on the LORD;
        the LORD answered me and set me in a broad place.

6   With the LORD on my side I do not fear.
    What can mortals do to me?
7   The LORD is on my side to help me;
    I shall look in triumph on those who hate me.
8   It is better to take refuge in the LORD
    than to put confidence in mortals.
9   It is better to take refuge in the LORD
    than to put confidence in princes.

10   All nations surrounded me;
    in the name of the LORD I cut them off!
11   They surrounded me, surrounded me on every side;
    in the name of the LORD I cut them off.
12   They surrounded me like bees;
    they blazed like a fire of thorns;
    in the name of the LORD I cut them off.
13   I was pushed hard, so that I was falling,
    but the LORD helped me.
14   The LORD is my strength and my might;
    he has become my salvation.

15   There are glad songs of victory in the tents of the righteous:
    "The right hand of the LORD does valiantly;
16   the right hand of the LORD is exalted;
    the right hand of the LORD does valiantly."
17   I shall not die, but I shall live,
    and recount the deeds of the LORD.
18   The LORD has punished me severely,
    but he did not give me over to death.

19   Open to me the gates of righteousness,
    that I may enter through them
    and give thanks to the LORD.

20   This is the gate of the LORD;
    the righteous shall enter through it.

21   I thank you that you have answered me
    and have become my salvation.
22   The stone that the builders rejected
    has become the chief cornerstone.
23   This is the LORD's doing;
    it is marvelous in our eyes.

24   This is the day that the Lord has made;
           let us rejoice and be glad in it.
25   Save us, we beseech you, O Lord!
           O Lord, we beseech you, give us success!

26   Blessed is the one who comes in the name of the Lord.
           We bless you from the house of the Lord.
27   The Lord is God,
           and he has given us light.
      Bind the festal procession with branches,
           up to the horns of the altar.

28   You are my God, and I will give thanks to you;
           you are my God, I will extol you.

29   O give thanks to the Lord for he is good,
           for his steadfast love endures forever.

This psalm shows considerable evidence of being a collection of liturgical materials from Israel's coronation procession. The evidences appear as we move through the text.

The psalm begins and ends (vv. 1, 29) with a call and a declaration that occurs frequently in the Psalms, a short formula that presents a central message of the entire Psalms volume. The call is "Give thanks to the Lord for he is good," and the declaration is "his steadfast love endures forever." This through the midst of all the struggle, the turmoil, the dispute, the fierce anger, the vengeance, the haughtiness, the violence, and the destruction to which the book of Psalms gives witness. These starting and ending verses accomplish two things. They connect Psalm 118 into the larger body of the Psalms, and they link up with the opening item of processional liturgy in verses 2-4. They are probably not liturgical items themselves.

Verses 2-4 show us the first piece of liturgy from the coronation procession. A strong voice from the procession, possibly the announcer at the beginning, would have shouted to the attending crowd, "Let Israel say, 'His steadfast love endures forever!'" whereupon all Israelites would have responded accordingly. The strong voice would have proceeded, "Let the house of Aaron say, 'His steadfast love endures forever!'" Those belonging to the priestly house of Aaron would have responded. The strong voice would have continued, "Let

those who fear the LORD say, 'His steadfast love endures forever!' "
The God-fearers, the Gentiles from other lands who worshiped Israel's
deity, would have made their proclamation. This at the head of the
procession was a way of beckoning everyone to attention.

Verses 5-18 are king-to-be-crowned words of the first order, articulated how and when in the procession we do not know. They
express the lowly, embattled estate from which the king has emerged,
the danger and distress of his beginnings. He has been surrounded
by many nations (vv. 10-12). He has been pushed hard, nearly to
the point of falling (v. 13). He has absorbed severe punishment (v.
18). But he has called on the Lord (v. 5). And in the name of the
Lord he has cut off the adversaries (v. 10). Repeatedly, in the name
of the Lord, he has cut them off (vv. 11-12). He knows that trust in
the Lord is better than putting trust in mortals (v. 8). The Lord alone
is his strength and his might (v. 14). Verses 15-17 are the ultimate
confession of the king's confidence in God. As a whole, these words
are a near-perfect articulation of Israel's plight against the ancient
Philistines and the giant Goliath, plus the subsequent emergence of
King David. I suspect that they originated in the telling of that story
and thus landed as liturgy in the coronation procession.

Verses 5-18 also display the evidences validating this kingship.
Though the adversaries were strong, he cut them off (v. 10). Though
they surrounded him, he cut them off (v. 11). Though they blazed like
a fire of thorns around him, he cut them off (v. 12). What stronger
validation could one ask for than victory over formidable enemies?

Verse 19 would have been spoken by the king-to-be as the procession reached Jerusalem's gate. It was, of course, addressed to the
gatekeepers.

Verse 20 was the gatekeepers' response as they opened the gate.

Verse 21 was the king's thankful prayer to God for bringing him
to this time and place, for delivering him to success and ascendance.

Verses 22-23, spoken by we-don't-know-whom, form a metaphorical story of the coronation and the history that has led up to
it. The metaphor was a well-known, popular one, often used in
describing Israel's emergence from slavery in Egypt. It also describes
their return from exile in Babylon: *We were nothing, discarded*
refuse on the trash heap of history, a useless piece of throwaway
rock. But the Lord raised us up as a cornerstone in God's great

building project. Such a "story" (myth) provides critically important meaning to any human community.

I wish for a better word than "marvelous" in verse 23. "Marvelous," in our language, originally meant wondrous, "filled with marvel." But now it usually means highly good, fantastic for me, greatly favorable to me. In this verse, it needs to return to its original meaning: incomprehensible, beyond our explanation. The term needs to be one that beckons you and me, not to feeling privileged and God-favored, but to humility and awe before the great Mystery.

Orally, in a classroom setting, Dr. James Sanders has suggested that the best translation of verse 24 is, "This is the day on which the Lord has acted! Let us rejoice and be glad in it!" The crowning of a king was a momentous *theological* event. The main thing going on was that God was reaching into human affairs to act. The Lord was touching Israel in this time and place. God did not do that on every whim, at every human beck and call. God acted among us when God acted. Without divine participation, the coronation ritual was an empty sham. Verse 24 declares that God was acting, a sacred moment. If so, it was full cause for gladness and rejoicing. We do not know who in the procession articulated these words.

Verse 25 was a prayer, possibly spoken by the same voice.

Verses 26-27 were declared by priests at the Jerusalem Temple, spoken or sung, as the procession grew near. They invited the crowd to place palm leaves and other leafy branches along the procession path.

Verse 28 was a declaration of faith spoken by the king, probably associated with the moment of crowning.

Thus does Psalm 118 make a substantial contribution to the coronation procession portrait that emerges across the Bible. Other texts, as we shall see, make others.

Psalms 96–100

Following closely after Psalm 89, which details the failure of the Davidic kingship line, the Psalms editors have placed Psalms 95–100, which proclaim in broad scope and strong voice that Israel's king is God. Of this cluster, Psalms 96–100 show evidence of having been used in association with a coronation procession.

The statement "he is coming . . ." (Pss 96:13, 98:9) is the first clue; the procession approaches. "Enter his gates with thanksgiving, and his courts with praise" (Ps 100:4) is the second clue as the procession enters the town gate and moves up to the Temple altar. But the main resonance here is with the spirited, universe-wide festivity. Throughout God's creation, every entity joins the celebration! The heavens are glad, and the earth rejoices; the sea roars, the field exults, the trees sing for joy (Ps 96:11-12). The sea roars, the floods clap their hands, the hills sing together for joy (Ps 98:7-8). All the earth makes a joyful noise (Ps 100:1). And throughout these psalms, people, near and far, are bidden to join the celebration: with songs of praise (Ps 98:4), with lyre and trumpet (Ps 98:5-6), with worship and ascription (Ps 96:7-9). Clouds and thick darkness surround him (Ps 97:2), fire goes out before him and consumes his adversaries (Ps 97:3), his lightnings light up the world, and the earth trembles (Ps 97:4). These were the accompaniments of an enthralling coronation procession for God. We do not know when or how often such processions were held, but they must have been huge community events.

Isaiah 40:3-5

In this text, dated in or shortly after 540 BCE, Israelite refugees are about to return from their Babylonian exile camp, across the desert, to Jerusalem. The prophet Isaiah declares, however, that this will not simply be a ragtag little herd of exiles trudging across the desert wilderness. It will be a coronation procession for God, Israel's now and future king. The journey may look humble and lowly to normal eyes, but Isaiah transforms it into a regal coronation! Elements from the standard coronation procession are clearly visible in his description.

In verse 3a, "A voice cries out: / 'In the wilderness prepare the way of the LORD. . . .' " This is the announcer at the procession's head, the one declaring to all what is happening.

In verses 3b-4, the royal procession route is being laid out. Instead of palm leaves and leafy branches on a road, however, the entire terrain will be refashioned to fit the occasion. ". . . make straight in the desert a highway for our God. / Every valley shall be lifted up, / and every mountain and hill be made low; / the uneven ground shall become level, / and the rough places a plain." God's coronation path is to be as fit-for-a-king as the creation can provide!

In verse 5, the crescendo occurs: "Then the glory of the LORD shall be revealed, and all people shall see it together. . . ." God's *glory*, in awesome splendor, will ride in the midst of the parade. We are not told of the vehicle, but little matter. All the ends of the earth will gather, multitudes from everywhere lining the procession route to shout acclaim. God has spoken this, Isaiah says, just as God spoke the creation into being in Genesis 1, and it will happen!

This scene, of course, is a strong exercise in prophetic imagination. Isaiah is proclaiming that through this very unspectacular human event, God will be working a magnificent cosmic event. While the people are doing one thing, God is doing something far greater. It takes special eyes to see what God is doing, what is *really* going on, but coronation processions, as we shall discover, seem particularly subject to double meaning.

The Gospel of Mark

The Gospel of Mark, written somewhere in the mid-60s CE, is, from beginning to end, an account of a coronation procession. The human beings in the story (except for one) are going about their normal, daily business of being human: becoming inspired by a persuasive leader, standing in awe at exceptional acts of power, being taught and teaching, being healed and healing, voicing vows of devotion, becoming jealous of one another, not "getting it," scoffing and deriding, becoming scared and afraid, forsaking vows, denying truths, fleeing in fear, and crucifying criminals. Those are all well within the human drama. God, according to Mark, employs these human acts to hold a coronation procession. All the standard procession elements appear; they provide the structure for Mark's gospel.

In his first public words (1:15), Jesus proclaims, "The time is fulfilled, and the kingdom of God has come near. . . ." This defines the subject of the book: God is visiting earth, and a coronation is about to unfold—for those with eyes to see. Mark will make clear, however, that the king to be crowned does not fit the standard pattern. In this gospel, a radical transformation in kingship emerges.

The announcer. The first event in Mark (1:3-8) is the appearance of John the Baptist, a voice "in the wilderness" (recall Isaiah 40:3) bidding Israel to prepare itself for a king's coronation. John is the clarion trumpet at the head of the procession.

The evidences. Very quickly after the announcer, Mark moves to a great aggregation of evidences that this king is God's choice. The evidences, however, are not booty gained through successful military conquest. They are victories over an unclean spirit at Capernaum (1:21-28), over Simon's mother-in-law's fever (1:30-31), over many illnesses and demon possessions (1:32-34), over leprosy (1:40-42), over paralysis (2:1-12), over the withering of a man's hand (3:1-5), over demon possession (5:1-20), over a little girl's death (5:21-24a, 35-43), over a woman's hemorrhages (5:24b-34), and over a small girl's demon possession (7:24-30). This progression continues through the healing of blind Bartimaeus (10:46-52), and then it abruptly stops; no more healings after that. Within these same chapters, Mark recounts further evidences for Jesus' kingship, the power and authority with which he taught, especially in the parables: of the sower (4:1-9, 13-20), of the lamp (4:21-25), of the growing seed (4:26-29), of the mustard seed (4:30-32); also, his teachings about temptations (9:42-48), about divorce (10:2-12), and about being rich (10:17-27).

Jesus stills a storm at sea (4:35-41), echoing God's power over "the waters" in Genesis 1:2. Jesus feeds the five thousand (6:30-44), echoing God's feeding of Israel in the Sinai wilderness (Exod 16). Jesus walks on the water (6:47-52). He is transfigured, his clothes becoming dazzling white, a voice declaring, "This is my son" (9:2-8): enormous validation that God is holding a coronation.

The king riding. Mark 11:1-10 tells of Jesus' ascending the eastern approach to Jerusalem, through Bethphage and Bethany, riding a donkey. "Many people spread their cloaks on the road," Mark says, "and others spread leafy branches that they had cut in the fields" (v. 8). Those who went ahead and behind shouted, "Hosanna [save us]! / Blessed is the one who comes in the name of the Lord! / Blessed is the coming kingdom of our ancestor David!" (vv. 9b-10a).

In Mark 11:11, Jesus enters the Jerusalem gate and proceeds to the temple.

The king's crown. In Mark 15:16-18, mocking soldiers clothe Jesus in a purple robe and twist thorns into a crown to place on his head. They salute him, declaring, "Hail, King of the Jews." To the humans, these acts are cynical derision; to God they are a coronation. The humans are working evil against a despised traitor; God uses their evil to work good for the perpetrators (recall the Joseph story, and especially Genesis 50:20—exactly the same dynamic).

The king's throne. In Mark 15:21-32, Jesus is raised up on a cross with an inscription of the charge against him, "The King of the Jews," precisely what the entire Gospel of Mark has been saying. His crucifixion has long been understood as his ascendance to a royal throne, high and lifted up—which is exactly Mark's message.

Mark's radical redefinition of Jesus' kingship is made quite clear in Mark 10:42-45. The disciples have been acting like typical humans, jockeying with one another to see who will be granted the highest status in his "glory." Jesus finally says to them,

> "You know that among the Gentiles those whom they recognize as their rulers lord it over them, and their great ones are tyrants over them. But it is not so among you; but whoever wishes to become great among you must be your servant, and whoever wishes to be first among you must be slave of all. For the Son of Man came not to be served but to serve, and to give his life as a ransom for many." (10:42-45)

The king in this coronation procession will rule not by commanding obedience but by serving, not with sword and cudgel but with compassion, not with arrogance but with humility. His kingdom will be not in a geographic region but in the depths of human hearts. He will make his residence not in a royal palace of pretense and privilege but in "Galilee" (Mark 16:7), amid struggling masses, where common humans labor and toil daily for their existence. He comes ". . . not to be served but to serve"—that is Mark's radical redefinition!

The Gospel of Luke

Luke, writing probably twenty years after Mark, uses Mark's basic coronation procession structure, but he elaborates the overall story considerably. Luke, too, is keenly aware of the dual character of gospel events: that they disclose what the humans were doing and also what God was doing. Luke's remarkable Emmaus Road story near the end (24:13-35) tells us that the twelve disciples themselves didn't really "get it" for a long, long time, until "their eyes were [finally] opened" (24:31).

In his triumphal entry narrative (19:29-40), Luke includes several unique features pertinent to our theme. He writes,

As he [Jesus] was now approaching the path down from the Mount of Olives, the whole multitude of the disciples began to praise God joyfully with a loud voice for all the deeds of power they had seen, saying,

"Blessed is the king
who comes in the name of the Lord!
Peace in heaven,
and glory in the highest heaven!"

Some of the Pharisees in the crowd said to him, "Teacher, order your disciples to stop." He answered, "I tell you, if these were silent, the stones would shout out." (19:37-40)

The first unique feature is the phrase "the whole multitude of the disciples." Since when do twelve people constitute a "whole multitude"? Even if their numbers swelled as they approached the city, they hardly would have constituted a whole multitude. In using the term, Luke is saying to us that this procession included "those who fear the LORD" (Gentiles) from Psalm 118:4; "all the earth" from Psalms 96:1, 98:4, and 100:1; "the nations" from Psalms 96:10 and 98:2; and "all people" from Isaiah 40:5, followers from many lands and places. This, indeed, was a God-instigated coronation procession!

Second, Luke reports (as Mark does not) that some Pharisees admonished Jesus, "Teacher, order your disciples to stop." Or, as the RSV translated it, "Teacher, rebuke your disciples." Those Pharisees were actually being very tolerant and generous. They could have had the entire assemblage arrested and put to death for sacrilege. Jesus' followers were mimicking a holy ritual, and the Jerusalem authorities, had they known, would have quashed the entire charade with full force. Jesus replied, "If these were silent, the stones would shout out!" (Luke 19:40). If the humans were quiet, the lifeless rocks along the roadside would burst their lungs in celebration, joining the heavens, the earth, the seas, the fields, the mountains, the trees, and the waves of Psalms 96–100! When God's coronation procession occurs, all of creation rejoices! It was this common awareness that Luke's message was tapping.

The gospels of Matthew and John also use the coronation procession structure, each, however, elaborating broadly in its own way. None of the noncanonical gospel writings employs this structure.

Philippians 2:5-11

⁵ Let the same mind be in you that was in Christ Jesus,
⁶ who, though he was in the form of God,
did not regard equality with God
as something to be exploited,
⁷ but emptied himself,
taking the form of a slave,
being born in human likeness.
And being found in human form,
⁸ he humbled himself
and became obedient to the point of death—
even death on a cross.

⁹ Therefore God also highly exalted him
and gave him the name
that is above every name,
¹⁰ so that at the name of Jesus
every knee should bend,
in heaven and on earth and under the earth,
¹¹ and every tongue should confess
that Jesus Christ is Lord,
to the glory of God the Father.

One other coronation procession is depicted in the New Testament. From the pen of the apostle Paul, it predates the earliest gospel, Mark, by around ten years.

Paul was writing a letter to the church he had founded in Philippi, a congregation toward which he seems to have had particularly warm feelings. He had stayed with that church for a period and then had moved on to other missionary endeavors. He was writing back to address a challenging question: now that Paul was gone, who was to guide the Philippian church in Christian living? How were they to resolve questions of behavior and ethics?

In the text quoted above, Paul is answering that question. He says: implant in your heads, screw into your brains, the mind given you by Christ Jesus. Think the way his life leads you to think. And here is how that is.

Jesus Christ, even though he was in the form of God (one with God in all respects), did not count his equality with God a thing to be tenaciously clutched, to be exploited, but, rather, he emptied himself. He set aside all divine prerogatives. He became a human. And not just any human but a servant human, one whose life is lived in the service of other people. And being found a human servant, he humbled himself even further by becoming obedient unto death. But not just any death; death on a cross, a criminal's death, the most lowly of all. In other words, as the Apostles' Creed says, "He descended into hell." Thus did he fully share our humanity, becoming one with us in our lowest estate.

Whereupon God highly exalted him and elevated him to royalty above all others. God set up a cosmic parade route that starts down below in the death world, extends upward through earth, and reaches into heaven. And God now runs a coronation procession along that route. The announcer announces ("at the name of Jesus"), and a huge throng gathers. Every knee in the throng bows and every tongue confesses "that Jesus Christ is Lord, / to the glory of God the Father."

Some scholars believe that this small bit of poetry was one of the first confessions of faith of the very early church. If so, it indicates clearly that the coronation procession was from the earliest Christian days a primary structure for interpreting the life of Jesus. Mark, in other words, was using a well-established, widely recognizable tradition in arranging his book. He didn't need to explain it because everybody understood it already.

The Point

Thus do we see that the Bible invites us to a royal parade, a cosmic celebration. In Psalm 118 is a liturgy used in a kings-of-Israel manifestation of that parade. Psalms 96–100 come from Jerusalem's celebration of God as king, after the Davidic kingship had fallen. Isaiah 40 presents another coronation procession for God as a band of exiles makes its way back across the desert toward its Jerusalem homeland. The Gospel of Mark lays out a full-blown coronation procession hidden within the seemingly mundane events of the life, travels, ministry, arrest, and crucifixion of Jesus of Nazareth. Luke plays further on this theme by having the entire creation take part, just as it does in Psalms 96–100. Paul in Philippians portrays the grand procession beginning in the underworld, the realm of death, extending through earth, and culminating in the realm of God.

The One being crowned is not a tyrant-ruler who lords it over subjects, demanding their obedience. The One being crowned is a servant: healing, teaching, feeding, stilling storms, casting out demons. That One is humble, appealing to the hunger for what is true and good that dwells in humans everywhere. That One rides the procession route, "full of grace and truth," and "we have seen his glory" (John 1:14-15).

It is a grand procession, believers of all nationalities, cultures, and skin colors taking part. The faithful from the past: Abraham and Sarah, Tamar, Moses, Ruth, David, the wise woman of Tekoa, Isaiah, Jeremiah, Elizabeth, Mary Magdalene, Peter, Paul, Augustine, Bernard of Clairvaux, John Calvin, Gandhi, Dietrich Bonhoeffer, Mother Teresa, Nelson Mandela, Archbishop Romero, and Martin Luther King Jr., to name but a few. The faithful present: Pope Francis, the Dalai Lama, Malala, Desmond Tutu, Melinda and Bill Gates, and untold others who devote their lives to human compassion and service. The faithful future, their names unknown to us, but we know they are in the throng. The hills are singing, the trees dancing, the waves clapping their hands, the stars lighting the world with sparkling brilliance, the fields rejoicing, earth and heaven echoing their refrains, and even the lifeless stones are shouting in proclamation. You can see it, hear it, feel it: the celebration! Across the universe reverberates the message: the king comes! The king comes!

And you and I are invited to join. We are welcomed into the crowd, chanting, singing, dancing, setting forth our palm leaves, clapping, and shouting. All we have to do is join the worship—there are plenty of options close by every week. As the "call to worship" is spoken, we will recognize the voice of the announcer coming up the hill. The royal entourage follows in all its magnificence: *the glory.* "Follow the One," the festivity beckons. "Make this king the ruler in your mind and heart and life."

All it takes is a bit of spiritual imagination, eyes to see, through mundane events, what is *really* going on.

Discussion Topics and Questions

1. Does our country value leaders who had humble beginnings? Can you name presidents or other significant leaders who arose out of low circumstances? What is it of value that we hope for in such people? What leadership qualities do we think they may have that more privileged people might not? Is it possible for a person born into wealth and privilege to empathize truly with those who were not?

2. "As dark approached, our doorbell rang and on the front stoop stood three small figures: Darth Vader, Wonder Woman, and Mickey Mouse." From that one sentence, tell me more. What did those three people say to you? Were you inclined to take their words literally, or did you have reason to know better? Name other things happening that evening. Where might you look to find a written description of these things? Name other happenings in our lives that no one would ever detail on paper because we all know about them already. Think about how some of these common rituals might be understood by interpreters two thousand years from now.

3. "The stone that the builders rejected / has become the chief cornerstone. / This is the LORD's doing; / it is marvelous in our eyes" (Ps 118:22-23). This, I suggested, was an expression of *Israel's story,* a metaphorical version of who they were and how they came to be. What would you say is the United States' story, the fundamental metaphor by which we understand ourselves? Several possibilities occur to me. *The exodus*: we are refuse from Europe and from across the world, brought here by God to be blessed with a land flowing with milk and honey. *A city set on a hill*: we are a light of opportunity, freedom, and goodwill, shining amid the darkness of many nations. *A melting pot*: we are humanity in all its many shapes, sizes, colors, cultures, and languages, set here to demonstrate the unity than can come from huge diversity. What metaphor do you think best tells our story? Which one describes the America you want this country to be? Identify people in our population who would tell our national story entirely differently from the way we do. What might they say? *A marauding menace*: people who have come from across the waters to steal our wealth and destroy our way of life? *Enslavers*: people who stole our freedom and our souls?

4. In the book *Hostage Bound, Hostage Free*, Ben Weir describes being abducted on a sidewalk in Beirut, Lebanon, placed in a room alone and chained to an iron radiator. In his solitude, he began treating the meals brought to him as the sacrament of communion. He would intone portions of the sacramental liturgy before eating and then surround himself, in his imagination, with fellow believers, people he knew across the world, naming their names and joining them in the sacramental celebration. This, he says, was a major tactic in his surviving his months of isolation: surrounding himself with a great crowd of friends through prophetic imagination. Have there been times in your life when you have brought distant companions and loved ones nearby through imagination? Can you describe a particular instance?

5. The next time you attend worship, think of yourself as standing on Jerusalem's eastern hill along the procession route for Christ's coronation. Name others there with you, and notice how the walls of the sanctuary in which you are worshiping have to swell vastly to contain the multitude. Hear the procession announcer, the call to worship. Hear the music, as the hills outside sing, the trees dance, the fields rejoice, the stars above you glisten, and the stones shout their praise. Think of how the whole creation comes to life in this moment! Consider the King being crowned: the people he healed, the crowds he fed, the teachings he taught, the acts he performed, the values he stood for, the way of thinking and living he offers to you. And then consider the specific call he extends to you, what this King bids you to do when he says, "Follow me." Commit yourself to something. *Make a promise* to do something new. The coronation procession can change your life!

CONCLUSION: THE BIG PICTURE

The Shape and Shaping of the Psalms

I end these studies with a sketch of the *big picture:* where our psalms came from, how 150 of them got selected and arranged into the book of Psalms, and the apparent overall intention of the editors. Having studied several separate units, we are now ready to fit pieces into a whole.

Where the Psalms First Came From

Somewhere around the time of King David, when Israel was yet a very young nation (David reigned from 1000 to 961 BCE), people were creating and singing psalms, music sung by individuals and in community gatherings expressing the emotions of the soul. Rejoicing and happiness, wonder and amazement, faith and hope, struggle and lament, bitterness and disillusionment, anger and vengeance: all of these found their way into music, as they do today. Song creation had been happening long before (we humans are that way), but it is from David's era that we can begin to document it.

The Role David Played

King David gained the reputation as the foremost psalm creator of ancient Israel. We do not know if he actually wrote psalms since we have no idea whether he could read and write, but David stands in the nation's tradition as the renowned author of psalms.

Others would follow; we don't know who or how many. But through the years and centuries of the kingdom (1000 to 587 BCE), others sang their way through whatever they were experiencing and shared their music with the community. Common practice in that time was to gather such verses under the label, "psalms of David," no matter their actual authorship. Thus are many labeled in our Bible. We can assume that some came from David while others did not. Distinguishing is impossible.

The Setting That Caused the Book of Psalms to Be Drawn Together

Repeating a bit from this book's introduction, 587 BCE was a pivotal year in Israel's life. The Babylonians destroyed Jerusalem and conquered the nation. Many, many Israelites were deported into exile in camps on the distant Euphrates River. Their home, their accustomed daily life, their theology, their national identity were all shattered, leaving a bleak future of subjection and servitude. Existing psalms were altered to reflect this new plight, and more (especially laments) were added.

Forty-seven years later, however, in 540 BCE Cyrus the Persian, who had conquered Babylon, told the Israelite exiles to go home. Cyrus, whose empire was booming east and west, held an enlightened attitude toward defeated nations, honoring their traditions instead of exiling and enslaving them. Thus did many Israelites make their way back across the desert to Jerusalem to begin rebuilding.

The Jerusalem temple was one of the rebuilding projects. After years of difficulties, the new temple was completed and dedicated in 515 BCE. In this time, the Psalms editors were working, selecting from music in the population's repertoire psalms that would go into the book. The 150 we have now became "the hymnbook of the second temple," complete with notations on how verses were to be sung. We do not understand those notations in the present day (*selah*, for instance).

The selection and arrangement were anything but random. The editors had a purpose, messages to deliver, images and impressions to convey, and the book of Psalms was constructed in accordance with that purpose. The chief purpose was to present a new Torah, a five-book set portraying the enormous struggles of how the nation came to be and God's instructions for its living—analogous to the first Torah. This Torah, however, would not detail events in the nation's history—the exodus, Sinai, etc.—but Israel's internal, spiritual journey: laments, yearnings, disillusionments, searches for meaning, continuing reconnection with God's creative power, declarations of God's love. This Torah would also lay out instructions on the ordering of the new nation's life, as had the first.

The fundamental message was that, just as God had acted to create the first nation of Israel, God was now acting to create the second, in essentially the same manner. God was once again raising up a people out of slavery and exile. God was bringing them through dangers and turmoils across a forbidding desert, led by the *glory*. And God was giving them a land. Everyone in 515 BCE believed that God had done this in the ancient past; full agreement there. The editors' challenge was to convince the people to believe it about *now*. "We are in a moment of God's visitation," the editors were saying, "when God has drawn close! Let us rejoice and take heart! God has winnowed Israel like wheat, purified it in the refiner's fire (to use prophetic images), and now God is ready to lead it forward toward a new righteousness, toward becoming an indestructible tree planted by streams of water!" This was the Psalms editors' message. The editors delivered it by fully acknowledging emotions from the recent past but then by setting in their place a new set of emotions (attitude) toward the future. Not a bad ambition for a hymnbook!

Viewing the Whole Book

Psalms begins with the editors' axiom of faith (Psalm 1): the righteous will prosper and grow strong; the wicked will be scattered as chaff in the wind. Those who live good lives will find reward; those who live evil lives will perish. Israel's whole future, the editors are saying, is grounded in this moral formula: obey and live; disobey and die.

Then follows a long series of laments questioning whether the axiom is true: the wicked too often prosper marvelously and receive grand accolades; the righteous too often suffer and are scoffed at. Lament psalm after lament psalm finds the wicked winning. These laments seem to reflect Israel's experience during its national disintegration of the late seventh century, Jerusalem's destruction, and the exile. Psalm 73 focuses all the laments, posing the key question in starkest terms: "Is Psalm 1 wrong? Should we be teaching children to do evil and wickedness rather than righteousness and good? Are we passing on to them a moral/theological lie?" Psalm 73 does not resolve the dilemma—the wicked continue to prosper—but it does resolve the psalmist's deep anguish. The psalmist visits the sacred places of God, experiences "the *glory*," soaks in holy awe, and knows thereafter who he must be and how he must live: in accord with Psalm 1. The *glory* has made clear who rules the universe and the direction it is moving: wickedness will be destroyed, God will walk with the righteous. *Living in the realm of grace*, this might be called, living in the faith that love accompanies us regardless of all else.

Anguish and lament continue in the Psalms, especially the great lament of Psalm 89 over the apparent collapse of God's covenant with David. But with Psalm 90 the psalmist invites Israel, from their deep mourning, to visit God's sacred places, to experience God's "from everlasting to everlasting" glory, and to continue forward.

Psalms 1, 73, and 89/90 are thus pivotal in the entire volume, marking the first half of the book. Their summary declaration is that wonder and amazement in God's sacred places are absolutely critical to faith, especially through severe struggle. This is why the Psalms editors have dotted glimpses of the *glory* throughout the book (Psalms 8, 19, 24, 65, 104, and 148), inviting the reader/singer to revisit it repeatedly. Psalms 22 and 23 declare that even through the worst hell, Presence always accompanies.

With Psalms 89/90, the book of Psalms makes an abrupt shift. God's covenant with David has been destroyed, and we enter a new era in the nation's life. The new era is actually a return to an old, old era, before Israel had a human king, when their only king was God. God's *glory*—a cloud by day and a pillar of fire by night—had led the nation forward through a great and terrible wilderness. This was in the era of Moses. Psalm 90, note, is the only psalm in the entire book attributed to Moses, marking the dawning of this age.

Psalms 93–100 (known as "the royal psalms") introduce this message in full: "God is king!" Psalms 101–103 extol God's virtues as royalty. Psalm 104 presents the new Genesis 1, a story of the grandeur, the "good," the Creator has set around us. Whereupon Psalms 105–107 depict *the gospel according to Psalms*, the essential dynamic of our relation to the Holy One.

Psalm 107 is of special import. "Steadfast love" becomes God's essential character, a quality that causes God not only to surround us with protective care but also to search us out from the farthest depths of difficulty and reclaim us. It is a clear message to exiles: from wherever you are, at the farthest reaches, the love of God, ever steadfast, is now coming forth to reclaim you. (This message will be repeated in Psalm 139. Notice also that Paul picks up the same theme in Romans 8, declaring that the steadfast love of God invades not only the farthest boundaries of earth but also the tombs in which we are laid, death itself, to enact its reclamation!) Psalm 107:42 resoundingly reaffirms Psalm 1: "The upright see it and are glad; and all wickedness stops its mouth." Whereupon verse 43 settles the issue: "Let those who are wise give heed to these things, and consider (ponder, 'meditate day and night') the steadfast love of the LORD." Living immersed in God's steadfast love becomes our life, our foremost experience of awe and the source of our instruction.

The psalms that follow (108–117) extol the greatness of God as Israel's leader. Psalm 118 is the liturgy from an Israelite coronation ceremony, now become the coronation of God. And the lengthy Psalm 119 is Israel's new commandment, urging wisdom, obedience, and wonder before the truth of God's holy instruction.

Psalms 120 and beyond return us to singing songs of Zion, God's sacred relationship with Israel and the holy city. Psalms 136–138 bring up the deepest of our vengeance and bitter hatred against our enemies, looking forward to the time when our own bitterness will be transcended by God's love. And after five prayers for deliverance (Psalms 140–144), Psalms 145–150 conclude the book of Psalms with a call for joyous, unending, resounding, unmitigated praise for God from every ounce of Israel's being and from every crevice of the universe. These psalms provide full amplification of the tiny verse appended at the end of the dispirited and mournful Psalm 89, "Blessed be the LORD forever. Amen and Amen" (v. 52), thus providing bookends for the entire latter half of the book. Psalm 89:52 is to become the song in Israel's heart, the center of her existence: "Blessed be the LORD God forever. Amen and Amen!"

God is visiting again, residing among us, traveling with us, the editors are proclaiming. No longer the cloud by day and pillar of fire by night, but now the *glory*. We wondered for a time if God had abandoned, withdrawn. No, God has brought us through the enslavement of exile, reclaimed us as God's own, and now promises our future. Come, Israel, move forward in this faith! "Blessed be the LORD forever! Amen and Amen" (Ps 89:52). "Let everything that breathes praise the LORD!" (Ps 150:6). "They (shall be) . . . trees planted by streams of water . . . , and their leaves do not wither." (Ps 1:3). That is the book of Psalms.